Star Billing

Star Billing

Tell-tale Trivia from Hollywood

David Brown

Weidenfeld and Nicolson
London

Published in Great Britain by
George Weidenfeld & Nicolson Limited
91 Clapham High Street
London sw4 7TA

ISBN 0 297 78696 2

Printed in Great Britain at The Bath Press, Avon

Contents

8

Six reasons for Marilyn Monroe's insecurity

Marilyn was born Norma Jean Mortensen – an illegitimate child.

Mrs Mortensen was deserted by both her husband and her lover at the time of Norma's birth. She suffered a nervous breakdown.

With the prior knowledge of Mrs Mortensen, a neighbour attempted to suffocate Norma at birth.

Norma was raped at the age of six by a friend of the family.

As a child, Norma lived with no less than twelve different families.

Norma spent some time in an orphanage where for scrubbing dishes and toilets, she was paid five cents a month.

... And one person who saw this insecurity at first hand

JUDY GARLAND

'I knew Marilyn Monroe and loved her deeply. She asked me to help her. Me! I didn't know what to tell her. One night at a party at Clifton Webb's house, Marilyn followed me from room to room.

'"I don't want to get too far away from you," she said. "I'm scared."

'"We're all scared," I replied. "I'm scared too."'

Three Oscar refusals

WOODY ALLEN
The diminutive former nightclub comedian refused to turn up to collect his Oscar for *Annie Hall* (1977), preferring to stay in New York playing jazz.

MARLON BRANDO
The Nebraska-born actor refused to accept his Best Actor Oscar for *The Godfather* (1972). Instead he sent a young Red Indian girl to the ceremony to plead the cause of her people.

GEORGE C. SCOTT
The mine-surveyor's son from West Virginia refused his Best Actor Oscar for *Patton – Lust for Glory* (1970). Nine years earlier when he heard that he had been nominated for Best Supporting Actor in *The Hustler* he asked to be withdrawn because he considered the Oscar ceremony 'Bull'.

Four actors whose screen image is at odds with their true personae

LEW AYRES
The star of the much acclaimed *All Quiet on the Western Front* (1930) became a conscientious objector in real life in 1941.

VICTOR MATURE
On the set of *The Robe* (1953), 'the Hunk' didn't run any risks of injury. One scene called for him to be clubbed, so the Props Department designed a special weapon. Though it looked solid it was really a sort of balloon. Mature was unimpressed – he was afraid it might burst.

SEAN CONNERY

Though James Bond likes his eggs boiled for three minutes and forty seconds, Sean Connery when confronted by an egg just pierces a hole in the top and sucks out the raw contents.

ERNEST THESIGER

The star of *The Bride of Frankenstein* was in real life a leading authority on embroidery.

Four actors whose lives were affected by women

RAY MILLAND

Ray Milland maintains that at the tender age of fourteen he was raped by a blonde girl of seventeen who had got him drunk at a party in Wales and had offered to give him a guided tour of her stables.

STEWART GRANGER

While Stewart Granger was on location filming *Captain Boycott* (1947) he maintains he was raped by a French woman who gave him the clap.

PETER FINCH

By the time he had reached the age of six Peter Finch had passed through the hands of three different women and had lived in two different countries. By the age of ten he had lived in England, France, Australia and India.

ROBERT MITCHUM

In the early 1980s, Robert Mitchum was forced to pay New York photographer Yvonne Hensley £200,000 after she claimed the star bounced a basketball off her face at an opening night film party, causing her considerable damage. Eye-witnesses stated that Mitchum was drunk at the time.

Three people who have fooled the public

COLONEL WILLIAM N. SELIG
The enterprising producer Colonel Selig hired a vaudeville actor with a slight resemblance to Theodore Roosevelt while the President was on safari in Africa in 1910. Then the producer made a movie of a lion hunt in his Chicago studio. The public accepted the end product as genuine.

ALFRED HITCHCOCK
Anthony Perkins was not on the set when the famous shower scene was filmed in *Psycho* (1960). The director, Alfred Hitchcock, went into the shower to deal the fatal blow.

GEORGE ROY HILL
In the famous cliff-jumping scene from *Butch Cassidy and the Sundance Kid* (1969), Robert Redford and Paul Newman jumped off the cliff on to a platform a few feet below the edge. The rest of the jump, made by two stuntmen, was filmed by the director, George Roy Hill, several weeks later in Malibu, Florida.

Sixteen miscellaneous quotes

'Sinatra could be terribly nice one minute and, well, not so nice the next. I was not impressed with the creeps and Mafia types he kept around him.'

PRINCE CHARLES ON FRANK SINATRA

'Anyone who has come close to Warren has shed quite a few feathers. He tends to maul you.'

LESLIE CARON ON WARREN BEATTY

'One thing about Steve, he didn't like the woman in his life to have balls.'

ALI MCGRAW ON STEVE MCQUEEN

'We never became lovers, but we could have – like that.'

SAL MINEO ON JAMES DEAN

'The lunatics have taken charge of the Asylum.'

RICHARD ROWLAND, HEAD OF METRO, *commenting in 1919 on the formation of the United Artists Corporation*

'In the long view of film history only talent means never having to say you are sorry.'

RICHARD CORLISS

'You're not a star until they can spell your name in Karachi.'

HUMPHREY BOGART

'Grant can milk more meaning out of a look, or a turn of his head, or just standing still, than most Hollywood hams can bludgeon out of fifty lines of dialogue.'

GEORGE JEAN NATHAN ON CARY GRANT

'She's silicone from the knees up.'

GEORGE MASTERS, MAKE-UP KING TO THE STARS, ON RAQUEL WELCH

'There was no love in my home. I was one of fifteen children, and the only physical contact I had with my mother was when she took me between her knees to pull lice out of my hair.'

CHARLES BRONSON

'There is a broad with a future behind her.'

CONSTANCE BENNETT ON MARILYN MONROE

'I can honestly say he's the most difficult actor I've ever worked with.'

NORMAN JEWISON, DIRECTOR, ON STEVE MCQUEEN

'A wide screen just makes a bad film twice as bad.'

SAMUEL GOLDWYN

'He's even-tempered – a personality trait not much in evidence among directors. The crew is totally behind him and that really helps things go smoothly.'

WILLIAM HOLDEN ON CLINT EASTWOOD

'Ronnie is really the only man I've ever known who loved dancing.'

DORIS DAY ON RONALD REAGAN

'"Too caustic?" To hell with the cost, we'll make the picture anyway.'

SAMUEL GOLDWYN

Seven generous deeds by the stars

A FILM
Peter Sellers produced a film at a cost of £6,000 starring Britt Ekland, Lord Snowdon and Princess Margaret (as Queen Victoria) and presented it to the Queen on her thirty-ninth birthday in 1965.

CREAM CAKES
James Mason and his wife spent £600 on cream cakes (at a cost of £100 a week) for the cast and crew of *Dr Fischer of Geneva*.

WAR RELIEF
Cary Grant gave over $100,000 to both British and American War Relief organizations.

RENT PAYMENT
There was a story in a British newspaper that a woman was about to be evicted from her home because of non-payment of rent. It was she who revealed that the cheque that saved her bore the signature of Frank Sinatra.

AN ISLAND
Raymond Burr, who himself has had a tragic private life (two wives died, a third divorced him and a son died of leukemia), bought a South Pacific island in order to provide a home for sixty deprived children.

A LOAN OF $1,500
In 1967 Donald Sutherland was a penniless out-of-work actor. In desperation he phoned Christopher Plummer and told him he wanted to go to America to look for roles to play, but unfortunately had no money. The following day Plummer's lawyer phoned and informed Sutherland that $1,500 had been placed in his account. It took Sutherland five years to repay the loan.

A MEMORABLE DINNER
Shortly after their first marriage Elizabeth Taylor and Richard Burton were being escorted to a table at one of New York's most fashionable restaurants when they overhead a receptionist informing a black couple: 'We're fully booked.' Burton and Taylor asked for a table for four and invited the black couple to join them.

Six people who have experienced the wrath of a star

AN AUTOGRAPH HUNTER
Silent movie star Norma Talmadge was approached by a fan a few years after her retirement in 1930 and asked for her autograph. 'Get away, dear,' the former star bellowed, 'I don't need you anymore.'

JAMES MASON ON RAQUEL WELCH
'I have never met anyone so badly behaved.'

A boxing fan

Sean Connery was sitting in a ringside seat watching the Henry Cooper–Cassius Clay fight when a woman stood in front of him and asked for his autograph. Connery was not amused. 'Get out of my bloody way, woman,' he shouted. 'Do you think I've paid fifty quid to sit here and look at you!'

Charles Laughton

Stewart Granger was so furious with Charles Laughton for scene stealing during the making of *Salome* (1953) that he told him that 'he would kick him in the balls if he didn't stop it'. Not surprisingly, Laughton relented.

A woman on the sidelines

On the set of *The Mirror Cracked*, Piers Brosnan, TV's Remington Steele, was filming a scene with Elizabeth Taylor in which she had to clasp him to her bosom and pant 'Jamie, Jamie'. In the middle of this emotional scene the multi-married Ms Taylor spotted a woman standing on the sidelines and snapped: 'Get that bitch out of my eyeline.'

Louis B. Mayer

At one of Louis B. Mayer's lavish birthday parties Perry Como got up and sang 'Happy Birthday, L.B., and fuck you!' Unfortunately for Como, he was blackballed from every studio in Hollywood for nearly five years.

... and one person who has reduced a star to hysterics

A writer

'From the moment I picked up your book until I laid it down I was convulsed with laughter. Some day I intend reading it.'

Groucho Marx

Four stars with financial acumen

W. C. FIELDS
The former tramp juggler once sold a story line which he had written on the back of an envelope for $25,000.

CARY GRANT
Once Cary Grant went to the news-stand at one of New York's leading hotels, picked up a magazine and handed the assistant half a dollar.

'That magazine is fifty-five cents,' the assistant told him.

'It says fifty on the cover,' Grant retorted.

'What difference does it make?' the assistant said. 'You've got it.'

'Yes, and that's how I got it,' replied Grant as he put the magazine back on the rack.

BEN TURPIN
The cross-eyed comedian took out insurance with Lloyd's of London against his eyes ever becoming uncrossed.

MONTGOMERY CLIFT
Stanley Kramer offered Montgomery Clift a key cameo role in *Judgement at Nuremberg* (1961). Clift's agent demanded his usual huge fee, so Clift did the part for nothing. He sent his agent an empty paper bag, containing, he said, his commission.

... and one star sadly without financial acumen

AL JOLSON
Warner Brothers offered Al Jolson stock in their company instead of a salary for his appearance in *The Jazz Singer* (1927). He demanded cash and thereby turned down a fortune.

Five stars the public has idolized

JAMES DEAN
Warner Brothers were still receiving 6,000 letters of mourning a year after the death of James Dean. Four million people became paying members of the James Dean posthumous Fan Club.

BOB HOPE
In 1977 De Von Smith travelled through forty-nine States in the USA to collect 100,000 signatures on Bob Hope's seventy-fifth birthday card.

SHIRLEY TEMPLE
When the child star Shirley Temple fell ill one year, 20,000 people on the island of Bali in Indonesia gathered on a vast field and fell to their knees in prayer for her recovery.

RUDOLPH VALENTINO
On the day of Valentino's funeral over 100,000 lined the streets of Los Angeles to pay homage to his funeral cortege.

RITA HAYWORTH
When Rita Hayworth's famous red locks were cut for *The Lady of Shanghai* a minister from Canada wrote to the hairdresser saying that cutting hair was against the teachings of the Bible. He closed by saying that it was the most beautiful hair he had ever seen and could he have some.

Two stories concerning Noel Coward

'RUNNING TADPOLES'
Noel Coward was staying in a hotel in Leningrad in the summer of 1939 when he turned on a tap in his bedroom and

saw to his amazement tadpoles streaming out instead of water. He sent for the manager and told him: 'In England when we want hot water, we turn on the tap marked "Hot". When we want cold water, we turn on the tap marked "Cold". When we want tadpoles, we turn on the tap marked "Tadpoles".'

A ROYAL LUNCHEON

At Queen Elizabeth's Coronation in 1953, Queen Salote of Tonga almost stole the show. Sitting beside this massive lady was a painfully thin Malaysian Sultan. When Noel Coward was asked by a friend who this gentleman was, he replied: 'Her lunch.'

Five tips from the stars

'A man tells the truth to a woman, a woman tells the truth to a man.'

Warren Beatty's recipe for an ideal relationship

'The secret is speed and the landing. You must beat the falling glass to the floor. It's much safer having glass falling on you, than you on it.'

Top stuntman Ray Austin, talking about jumping through windows

When Elizabeth Taylor is dieting she has coffee for breakfast, scrambled egg for lunch and steak for dinner. When she has a craving for something sweet she puts chocolate cake in her mouth for a few minutes but always removes it before swallowing.

While on tour in 1949 with Tolstoy's *The Power of Darkness*, Stewart Granger, during a curtain speech in Grand National Week, advised the audience to back a 50-1 chance called 'Russian Hero' for the race because they had just seen a Russian play in which he played the hero. The horse duly obliged.

Errol Flynn used as an aphrodisiac a pinch of cocaine at the end of his penis.

Three stars with healthy sexual appetites

HEDY LAMARR
Hedy Lamarr once propositioned Stewart Granger in a hotel room in Marseilles. She is reported as saying: 'Kings want to. Heads of studios want to. Presidents want to. Why don't you want to?' The nervous Granger, after his initial trepidation, accepted the offer but changed his mind when the Austrian-born actress told him: 'Now don't come too fast.'

FREDRIC MARCH
Standing by his dressing room door, Fredric March was once asked what he would have done if he hadn't been an actor. All of a sudden he grabbed a blonde starlet and said: 'I wanted to be a banker, but this is more fun.' With that he returned to his dressing room with the actress and locked the door.

MARILYN MONROE
'Marilyn Monroe went to bed with half of Hollywood, including Brando, Sinatra and the members of the Kennedy family – JFK and Bobby. Strangely she was a sex symbol who didn't care too much for sex.'

Sheilah Graham

Ten stars on 'Sex'

SARAH MILES
'The trouble with sex is that it so often leads people to develop huge fantasies about each other.'

DUDLEY MOORE
'I'd rather be dead than give up sex. Sex is the most important thing in life for me.'

MERYL STREEP
'Everybody can make out, but not everybody can feel the real thing.'

CARY GRANT
'The trick is to be relaxed; if you can attain true relaxation you can make love for ever.'

WARREN BEATTY
'If I tried to even keep up with what was said about me sexually, I would be, as Sinatra once said, "Speaking to you from a jar in the University of Chicago Medical Centre".'

CLARK GABLE
'Hell, if I'd jumped on all the dames I'm supposed to have jumped on – I'd never have had time to go fishing.'

ELIZABETH TAYLOR
'I think sex is absolutely gorgeous. I don't make any bones about sex being wonderful. Anyone who says it isn't is either mentally sick or afraid he or she can't measure up.'

VIVIEN LEIGH
'I am an actress,' Vivien Leigh once told a friend, 'a great actress. Great actresses have lovers, why not? I have a husband and I have lovers. Like Sarah Bernhardt.'

JOAN COLLINS
'People seem to think that if you've had more than two or three men in your life you must be a whore.'

MARIA SCHNEIDER

Maria Schneider, the actress who starred with Marlon Brando in *Last Tango in Paris*, has admitted: 'I'm a bisexual completely.'

Ten notable firsts

Dirk Bogarde was probably the first major screen star to accept the part of a homosexual in the first ever film to deal mainly with the subject, *Victim* (1961).

The first public appearance of a movie was at the 'Koster and Bials' Music Hall in New York on 23 April 1896.

The first animated film was *Gertie the Dinosaur* (1909), drawn by Winsor McCay.

The first movie to be screened at the White House was *The Birth of a Nation* (1915), starring Lillian Gish.

The first full-length all-talkie film made in Great Britain was *Blackmail* (1929).

Laurence Olivier became the first actor to be made a Life Peer in 1970.

The first man on the movie moon landed in *Rocket on the Moon* (1902).

The first star to produce her own film was Helen Gardner.

The first film with synchronized music and effects was *Don Juan* (1926).

Lauren Bacall's first words on screen were 'Have you got a light?' in *To Have and Have Not* (1944).

Four personalities who have been sacked

THE DIRECTOR
The Austrian director Erich Von Stroheim was sacked by Universal mogul Irving Thalberg for ordering silk underwear, with the monogram of the Imperial Guard, for the guardsmen when filming *Merry-Go-Round* (1923), even though they would never be shown in anything less than full uniform. Thalberg was also unimpressed when he heard that Stroheim had spent three whole days teaching extras how to salute in the correct Austrian manner.

THE SCREENWRITER
Scott Fitzgerald was sacked from his job as screenwriter for the film *Raffles, the Amateur Cracksman* (1940) for writing the following dialogue:
Raffles (David Niven) : 'Smile.'
Girl (Olivia De Havilland) : (Smiles.)
Raffles : 'Wider.'
Girl : (Smiles wider.)
Raffles : 'I'm going to ask you a very important question.'
Girl : 'Oh, darling!'
Raffles : 'Tell me . . . who is your dentist?'

THE ACTOR OR THE PRODUCER?
George Lazenby, who briefly flirted with fame as James Bond in *Her Majesty's Secret Service* (1969), believes that he is very misunderstood. 'I was looked upon as a failure. Everybody thought that I had failed because the producer Cubby Broccoli, fired me but the truth of the matter is that I fired him!'

THE WRITER
Harry Cohn, head of Columbia Pictures, was boasting at a lunch party that he always knew when he had a good film. Even when he was alone in his private projection room he had a fool-proof device for judging the merits of a film. 'If my fanny

squirms, it's bad, if it doesn't it's good. It's as simple as that.'
There was a short silence, then writer Herman Mankiewicz
joked: 'Imagine the whole world wired to Harry Cohn's arse.'
He was sacked on the spot.

Six energetic stars

JOHN WAYNE
The archetypal American hero appeared in more Hollywood
films than any other star.

ROBERT SHAW
The actor and novelist fathered ten children from his three
marriages.

MAX STEINER
The Austrian composer was nominated twenty-six times for
the Oscar for Best Score. His work included *Gone with the Wind*
(1939) and *Casablanca* (1942).

STELLA STEVENS
The actress who was photographed nude by Playboy in the
1960s was married at fifteen, a mother a year later and divorced
at seventeen.

WARREN BEATTY
'He (Warren Beatty) was insatiable. Three, four, five times a
day, every day was not unusual for him, and he was also able to
accept phone calls at the same time.'

ex-lover Joan Collins

ELVIS PRESLEY
The singer/actor saw *King Solomon's Mines*, starring Stewart
Granger and Deborah Kerr, sixty times.

Two fatal car crashes

JAMES DEAN
On 30 September 1955 James Dean, driving his Silver Porsche Spider at 86 mph, collided with another car at the intersection of Routes 466 and 41 near Paso Robles, California. He died instantly.

JAYNE MANSFIELD
In 1967 the busty star was on her way to a television engagement accompanied by her fiancé. They were both decapitated when their sports car was involved in an accident with a lorry near New Orleans.

...And one lucky escape

MONTGOMERY CLIFT
In May 1956 Montgomery Clift crashed on his way home from a dinner party, wrapping his car around a tree. He completely shattered his jaw, broke his nose and two teeth lodged in his throat. Fellow party guest Elizabeth Taylor somehow reached down and extracted the teeth, thereby saving his life.

Four stars who suffer from shyness

GRETA GARBO
'Making a film with Garbo,' said Robert Montgomery, 'does not constitute an introduction.'

DORIS DAY
According to Doris Day's autobiography her three husbands variously beat her, cheated her and deserted her. Not

surprisingly, she now lives as a recluse in the Cartmel Valley, California.

WALTER MATTHAU
'I've overcome my shyness with a façade of professional horseshit.'

DEANNA DURBIN
Deanna Durbin, who for more than twelve years was a massive Hollywood star, suddenly at the age of twenty-eight went to live in France, where she has remained, living the life of a recluse. She once said: 'I'm fed up with all the ballyhoo. I would prefer to be forgotten.'

Five stars' hopes for the future

'Some day I would like a part where I can lean my elbow against a mantelpiece and have a cocktail.'

CHARLES BRONSON

'To figure out how I can responsibly use what money I earn and what fame I have to improve the quality of people's lives.'

JANE FONDA

'To star in a musical. I think I am a singer.'

ALAN BATES

'For other people to see how much animals suffer.'

BRIGITTE BARDOT

'I want to do Macbeth – naked.'

WALTER MATTHAU

David Brown's top ten films of all time

1 *The Thirty-nine Steps* (1935 version).
2 *Kind Hearts and Coronets.*
3 *Some Like It Hot.*
4 *Brief Encounter.*
5 *California Suite.*
6 *Bringing up Baby.*
7 *Psycho* (1).
8 *To Catch a Thief.*
9 *The Graduate.*
10 *Strangers on a Train.*

The nationality of ten stars

Charles Bronson	*Lithuanian.*
Yul Brynner	*Mongolian.*
Tony Curtis	*Half Hungarian.*
Stewart Granger	*British.*
Audrey Hepburn	*Irish/Dutch.*
Deborah Kerr	*Scottish.*
Yves Montand	*Italian.*
Sylvester Stallone	*Half Sicilian.*
Anthony Quinn	*Irish/Mexican.*
Peter Ustinov	*White Russian.*

Ten of the more long-lasting Hollywood marriages

Mel Brooks and Anne Bancroft	1964–
Gary Cooper and Veronica Balfe	1933–1961

27

Douglas Fairbanks Jnr and Mary Lee	1940–
Glenn Ford and Eleanor Powell	1943–1959
Bob Hope and Dolores Reade	1934–
Burt Lancaster and Norma Anderson	1947–1969
Walter Matthau and Carol Wellington-Smythe-Marcus	1959–
Steve McQueen and Neile Adams	1957–1972
Robert Mitchum and Dorothy Spence	1940–
James Stewart and Gloria McLean	1949–

... And one of Hollywood's shortest marriages

Debra Paget's marriage to director Budd Boetticher lasted just twenty-two days.

Seven stars who married well

Dawn Adams	Prince Vittorio Massimo.
Sylvia Hawks	Lord Ashley.
Rita Hayworth	Prince Aly Khan.
Grace Kelly	Prince Rainier of Monaco.
Peter Lawford	J.F. Kennedy's sister Patricia.
Marilyn Monroe	Arthur Miller (Pulitzer Prize Winner).
Gloria Swanson	Marquis de la Falaise de la Coudraye.

Seven stars who could justly be labelled eccentric

MARIO LANZA
As well as having a vast appetite for women, drink and drugs, the great singer hardly ever washed and never bothered to relieve himself in the proper places.

CORINNE GRIFFITH

In the mid 1960s Corinne Griffith claimed in a divorce court that the real Corinne had died in her thirties and that she, her stand-in, had replaced her in all her sound films.

MONTGOMERY CLIFT

When on location filming *Raintree County* (1957) for MGM there were two occasions when Montgomery Clift was discovered wandering around outside, in the middle of the night, naked.

SARAH MILES

Sarah Miles one day turned up on the set of *Ordeal by Innocence* wearing a smart pair of boots. When a member of the film crew admired them the actress remarked that they were 'Gladys – my late Skye terrier.'

PETER O'TOOLE

The star of *Lawrence of Arabia* always wears green socks, never wears a watch, never carries a wallet and never takes house keys with him. 'I just hope some bastard's in.'

SUE LYON

The actress who played Lolita in 1963 eleven years later married a man serving a forty-year jail sentence for murder. The following year she filed for divorce.

HEDY LAMARR

The day before John Loder was due to marry Hedy Lamarr in May 1942 he received a letter from her enclosing a bill for three hundred and fifty dollars. She said that it was exactly half the price of the food and wine they had consumed together at her home. Loder wrote out a cheque and the marriage went ahead.

Nine brainy stars

DEGREES
Richard Burton read Classics at Oxford University. Dyan Cannon has a degree in Anthropology from the University of Washington. Peter Falk ('Columbo') has an MA in Public Administration and a BA in Political Science. Vincent Price has a degree in Art History and English from Yale and a degree in Fine Arts at London University.

LINGUISTS
Elke Sommer is fluent in seven languages. Edward G. Robinson could converse effortlessly in eight different tongues. Stephanie Powers speaks seven languages as well as being an expert on European art.

CHILD GENIUS
Robert Mitchum could read and write by the age of three.

DECEPTIVE
'Montgomery Clift was an exceptionally bright man who liked to pretend he wasn't, unlike Marlon Brando who likes to pretend he's bright whereas in fact he isn't really.'

Edmund Dmytryk

Eight famous people who have delivered a funny line

NOEL COWARD
When Noel Coward was in Hollywood he learnt of the suicide of an actor friend of his who had a reputation for not being terribly bright.

'How did he kill himself?' Coward asked.

'He shot his brains out,' he was told.

'He must have been a marvellous shot,' commented Coward.

WOODY ALLEN

Woody Allen was once asked what he'd like to come back as in another life. He replied: 'Warren Beatty's fingertips.'

PETER O'TOOLE

When Peter O'Toole was doing National Service he was given a written test to discover whether he was of officer potential. Of the twenty questions asked he only answered one – How would he lift a heavy barrel over a thirty-foot wall with two ten-foot lengths of rope? O'Toole's answer was: 'I'd call the Chief Petty Officer over and say to him "get that barrel over the wall."'

JOHN WAYNE

Once a man shouted from a crowd to John Wayne asking him if he spoke Spanish.

'Not too well,' replied Wayne.

'What! You've had three Spanish wives and you can't speak Spanish?'

'Waal,' drawled Wayne, 'I guess I just never listened to them.'

WALTER MATTHAU

After Walter Matthau had had a heart attack he said: 'My doctor gave me six months to live but when I couldn't pay the bill, he gave me six months more.'

Once the star burst into his bedroom to find his wife Carol in bed with their young son Charlie. 'Don't move anyone,' he shouted, 'I'm sending for Freud.'

THE QUEEN

When Queen Elizabeth II met Hollywood producer Ross Hunter, she said to him: 'I want to tell you, Mr Hunter, that I liked your *Flower Talk* and *Drum Song* very much.' Then she added in a whisper: 'But I loved your *Pillow Talk*.'

Mr Krushchev

When the Soviet Premier visited Twentieth Century Fox, Spyros Skouras gave a speech saying that the United States was a great country where a poor Greek immigrant, like himself, could rise to be President of Twentieth Century Fox. Khrushchev replied that Russia was greater than the United States because a poor peasant like himself could rise to be President of an even greater company, the USSR.

Alfred Hitchcock

When the celebrated English director was asked what he would like on his tombstone, he replied: 'You can see what can happen to you if you aren't a good boy.'

... And one star who was broad-minded

In an interview David Frost asked Paul Newman what he and his wife Joanne Woodward had in common. Newman replied: 'Absolutely nothing. But she's a good broad.'

Five people who discovered that first impressions can be misleading

The cameraman on Sophia Loren's screentest in 1951:
 'She is quite impossible to photograph, too tall, too big-boned, too heavy all around. The face is too short, the mouth is too wide, the nose is too long. What do you want of me, miracles?'

A Paramount Executive to Cary Grant (after his first screentest):
 'You're bow-legged and your neck is far too thick.'

Time magazine on Walter Matthau:
  'He is about as likely a candidate for superstardom as the neighbourhood delicatessen man.'

Jack Warner to Clark Gable after a Warner Brothers screentest:
  'You're only a big ape.'

Studio report on Fred Astaire's first screentest:
  'Can't act, can't sing. Can dance a little.'

Five memorable cables

'Dear Mike, don't die yet, it's my turn first.'
  A cable received by Michael Wilding, when he was in hospital and reported dying, from ex-lover Marlene Dietrich.

'I need you, come at once. You will know why when you read the headlines in the morning papers.'
  Ava Gardner was in London filming *Mayerling* when she received this cable from ex-husband Frank Sinatra, who had just announced his separation from Mia Farrow. Miss Gardner dropped everything and immediately flew out to Mexico. She was far from pleased on reaching Sinatra's hotel, to be informed that he had already checked out.

'When I was a boy in Russia your police treated my people very badly. However, no hard feelings. Hear you are out of work. Glad to offer you job with me. Regards.'
  The contents of a cable sent by Lewis J. Selznick, producer, to the ex-Tsar, Nicholas II, after the February Revolution.

'She is and always will be a star, one we shall never forget, nor cease to be grateful for.'
  A cable received by Clark Gable in 1942 from President Roosevelt upon the tragic death of his wife, Carole Lombard, in a plane crash.

Harry Cohn, head of Columbia Studios, sent a frantic cable to the director, Lewis Milestone, in the middle of production of *The Captain Hates the Sea*.

'Hurry up!' the cable read. 'The cost is staggering!'

Milestone cabled back:

'So is the cast.'

The cast included such notorious tipplers as John Gilbert and Victor McLaglen.

Ten stars' former jobs

Warren Beatty	*Rat-catcher.*
John Barrymore	*Cartoonist.*
Barbra Streisand	*Switchboard operator.*
Clint Walker	*Deputy sheriff in Las Vegas.*
Walter Matthau	*Boxing instructor.*
Oliver Reed	*Strip club bouncer.*
Rudolph Valentino	*Gardener, gigolo, dishwasher.*
Rita Hayworth	*Spanish dancer in Mexican nightclubs.*
Clint Eastwood	*Army swimming instructor.*
Kirk Douglas	*Parking lot attendant, professional wrestler.*

Ten stars of musicals who didn't sing

Rita Moreno	*West Side Story.*
Deborah Kerr	*The King and I.*
Ava Gardner	*Showboat.*
Lana Turner	*The Merry Widow.*
Christopher Plummer	*The Sound of Music.*
Rosalind Russell	*Gypsy.*

Leslie Caron	*Gigi.*
Audrey Hepburn	*My Fair Lady.*
Cyd Charisse	*Brigadoon.*
Rita Hayworth	*Cover Girl.*

... And two particularly odd voice-overs

Lauren Bacall (by Andy Williams) in *To Have and Have Not.*
Larry Parks (by Al Jolson) in *The Jolson Story.*

Six angry remarks about changes in the cinema

'Goddamit, can't they realize that most movie-goers are sick to death of the dingy sexpot who lives next door and the hairy oaf who's screwing her.'

RAY MILLAND

'There aren't any real movie-makers any more. The business is run by the cornflakes men and they are only in it for the girls. You used to join amateur dramatics to get at the crackling. These men buy up studios to achieve the same end. You see them flying around in their private jets with birds. We used to hide under the table fifteen years ago. It's insane. Crackling should be an added bonus, not an end in itself.'

PETER O'TOOLE

'My interest in the cinema has lapsed since women began to talk.'

GEORGE JEAN NATHAN IN A LETTER TO JAMES AGATE

'I am really appalled by some of the public exhibitions on the screen by good actors and actresses who certainly have the talent to convey the impact of what they are doing without showing us to the last detail of pubic hair and rosy nipple how they are doing it.'

DORIS DAY

'I don't care for modern films. Cars crashing over cliffs and close-ups of people's feet.'

LILLIAN GISH

'I don't want to read about some of the actresses who are around today. They sound like my niece in Scarsdale. I love my niece in Scarsdale, but I wouldn't buy tickets to see her act.'

VINCENT PRICE

Eleven comments on Hollywood

'Hollywood is not a place, it's a state of mind.'

WILTON MIZNER

'They know only one word of more than one syllable here, and that is fillum.'

LOUIS SHERMAN

'Hollywood is a community of lonely people searching for even the most basic kind of stimulation in their otherwise mundane lives.'

ROD STEIGER

'Hollywood is a place where people from Iowa mistake each other for stars.'

FRED ALLEN

'Strip away the phoney tinsel in Hollywood and you find the real tinsel underneath.'

OSCAR LEVANT

'There used to be chiefs, now there are only Indians.'

ROSS HUNTER

36

'Hollywood is the town where inferior people have a way of making superior people feel inferior.'

DUDLEY FIELD MALONE

'Hollywood is like Picasso's bathroom.'

CANDICE BERGEN

'I look upon going to Hollywood as a mission behind enemy lines. You parachute in, set up the explosion, then fly out before it goes off.'

ROBERT REDFORD

'Hollywood is divided into two groups. Those who do cocaine and those who don't.'

TERENCE YOUNG

'Hollywood is a strange place. Everyone is looking for a formula. One year it's the guys on a motorcycle, the next it's a girl dying of cancer. For years, I bummed around trying to get a job and it was the same old story – my voice was too soft, my teeth needed capping, I squinted too much and I was too tall. All that tearing down of my ego, it was bound to turn me into either a better person or a bastard.'

CLINT EASTWOOD

Five stars who admitted to homosexuality

MONTGOMERY CLIFT
His excessive drinking was said to be caused by guilt over his homosexuality. After 1957 he was 'so drunk that he couldn't work afternoons'.

RAINER WERNER FASSBINDER
The famous German director, though briefly married, proclaimed his homosexuality both on and off the screen.

RICHARD BURTON
In 1975 Richard Burton told David Lewin that he drank
because he had once been a homosexual.

ALAIN DELON
In 1969 Delon admitted on British TV to the amazement of his
legions of female fans that he had once been a homosexual.

CHARLES LAUGHTON
Perhaps the greatest British character actor of them all,
Laughton was a homosexual, though he was happily married
to actress Elsa Lanchester for many years.

...And one lady who had an affair with a homosexual

Marilyn Monroe had an affair with a young homosexual
during the time she was working on *There's No Business Like
Show Business*, 'to make him feel like a man'.

The age they'd be if they were still alive in 1985

Montgomery Clift	64
James Dean	54
Robert Donat	80
Judy Garland	63
Boris Karloff	98
Charles Laughton	86
Vivien Leigh	72
Marilyn Monroe	59
Elvis Presley	50
Peter Sellers	60

Ten unbelievable film titles

How to stuff a wild bikini
Brother Rat and a Baby
Won Ton Ton, the Dog that Saved Hollywood
Duck, You Sucker
Is Your Honeymoon Really Necessary?
Hallelujah, I'm a Bum
Blakula and Blackenstein
Are You a Mason?
The Sterile Cuckoo
Ah, Wilderness!

Five odd conversations

WALTER MATTHAU AND A GIRL IN THE STREET
Walter Matthau once went up to a girl and said: 'How old are you? Do you want to make love? To the actor's astonishment the girl readily agreed to the proposition. 'No, no, I was just showing off my new freedom, my liberation from the shackles of ignorance, despair and darkness,' cried Matthau. 'Oh,' she said, disappointed. 'I thought you were serious.'

LAUREN BACALL AND THE SHAH OF IRAN, NEW YEAR'S EVE 1956
Shah of Iran: 'You are a wonderful dancer, Miss Bacall . . . you must have been born to dance.'
Lauren Bacall: 'You bet your arse, Shah.'

LANA WOOD AND WARREN BEATTY
In her memoirs Lana Wood recalls that shortly after her sister, Natalie Wood, drowned she went to see Warren Beatty, only for him to make a pass which she rejected. Surprised at this

behaviour from Natalie's ex-lover she asked him: 'Do you miss Natalie?'

To which Beatty replied: 'No, not really. She's gone and I'm sorry and that's it.'

SPENCER TRACY AND A REPORTER
A reporter once asked Spencer Tracy: 'Aren't you tired of always playing Tracy?'

To which the great man replied: 'What the hell am I supposed to do – play Bogart?'

FRANKIE HOWERD AND ZSA ZSA GABOR, 1972
Frankie Howerd: 'You must give many interviews?'
Zsa Zsa Gabor: 'Ach, in seven languages.'
Frankie Howerd: 'Seven?'
Zsa Zsa Gabor: 'Seven. Mind you darlink, all lies.'

Six stars who weren't enamoured by the finished product

Ray Milland on *Love Story*: 'As a result of a mis-spent life, I was given the role as the father.'

Bette Davis on *Beyond the Forest*: 'A terrible movie', in which she played 'the longest death scene ever seen on the screen.'

Paul Newman on *The Silver Chalice*: 'The worst film of the Fifties.'

Frankie Howerd on *The Cool Mikado*: 'I can say without equivocation that not only was it the worst film ever made but the only production in show business that I'm positively ashamed of having appeared in.'

Burt Lancaster on *Airport 1969*: 'The biggest piece of junk ever made.'

Richard Harris on *Mutiny on the Bounty* (1962): 'The whole picture was just a large, dreadful nightmare for me.'

... And one actress who was physically sick

After seeing the British première of *Cleopatra* in 1963, Elizabeth Taylor, who played the title role, was sick in the downstairs lavatory of the Dorchester Hotel.

The all-time list of top movie stars (1932–1980)

1 John Wayne.
2 Betty Grable.
3 James Stewart.
4 Elizabeth Taylor.
5 Shirley Temple.
6 Steve McQueen.
7 Spencer Tracy.
8 Mickey Rooney.
9 Robert Redford.
10 Barbra Streisand.

(From information given in *Variety* and from the *Motion Picture Almanacs*.)

Roger Vadim on four women in his life

BRIGITTE BARDOT
'She saw life with me as a cake called "Happiness" which she could eat day and night, winter and summer, awake or asleep.'

ANNETTE STROYBERG
'I had been her genie, covering up her weaknesses and giving her time to learn, but she believed in illusions and refused to admit that her success was due only to luck and good looks.'

CATHERINE DENEUVE
'Soon my shy adolescent had blossomed out into a hard-headed woman ruthlessly in control of her life.'

JANE FONDA
'Humour is not one of Jane's strong points, and she usually fails to grasp a point unless it is stated explicitly.'

Twelve stars who didn't particularly enjoy working with each other

JANE FONDA ON LAURENCE HARVEY
'Acting with Harvey is like acting by yourself – only worse.'

TREVOR HOWARD ON ANITA EKBERG
'I thought there was something more worthwhile in life than acting with an ex-Beauty Queen.'

BARBRA STREISAND AND WALTER MATTHAU
During the filming of *Hello Dolly*, Barbra Streisand referred to co-star Walter Matthau as 'Old sewer mouth' and he called her 'Miss Ptomaine'. 'I had no disagreement with Barbra Streisand. I was merely exasperated at her tendency to be a complete megalomaniac,' Matthau said later. When asked whether he would like to work with Barbra Streisand again, he replied: 'I'd love to work with Barbra Streisand again in something appropriate, perhaps *Macbeth*.'

KIRK DOUGLAS ON BURT LANCASTER

'I've finally got away from Burt Lancaster. My luck has changed for the better. I've got pretty girls in my pictures now.'

DORIS DAY ON KIRK DOUGLAS

'The film I made with Kirk, *Young Man With a Horn*, was one of the few utterly joyless experiences I had in films.'

JOAN COLLINS ON GEORGE PEPPARD

'He's arrogant – the sort of man who expects women to fall at his feet at the slightest command; who throws his weight around. He gives the impression that he's the star, what he says goes and that nobody else is very important.'

The humour of Joan Rivers

ON ELIZABETH TAYLOR

'They say black makes you thinner – so she should hang out with the Supremes.' 'More chins than the Chinese phone book.'

ON BO DEREK

'Out to lunch as far as I am concerned. The woman is an idiot, she turned down the role of Helen Keller – she couldn't remember the lines.'

ON JANE FONDA

'Jane's got a good body. But God gives and God takes away – she's got to sleep with Tom Hayden.'

ON HERSELF

'I'm such a bad housekeeper people wipe their feet before they leave. My body is so bad a Peeping Tom looked in my window and pulled down the shade.'

The five regrets of John Huston

In John Huston's autobiography *An Open Book* (1980) he says that if he had his life again:
  'I would spend more time with my children.'
  'I would make more money before spending it.'
  'I would learn the joys of wine instead of hard liquor.'
  'I would not smoke cigarettes when I had pneumonia.'
  'I would not marry a fifth time.'

Six actors name their own particular favourites

'Walter is a helluvan actor. The best I've ever worked with.'
    JACK LEMMON ON WALTER MATTHAU

'Not just a great actor but a genius.'
    ROGER VADIM ON MARLON BRANDO

'When you've danced with Cyd Charisse you stay danced with.'
    FRED ASTAIRE

'I consider Peter Finch and James Mason the two best English actors of the 1960s. But I never understood Finch. How could he do something as beautiful as *Sunday, Bloody Sunday*, but also make all that other shit? I mean he could read, couldn't he?'
    ALAN BATES

'I was never in love with any woman as deeply as I was with Sophia.'
    PETER SELLERS ON SOPHIA LOREN

'The finest actress I have ever worked with.'
    BURT LANCASTER ON SHIRLEY BOOTH

Four stars who were conscious of their image

YUL BRYNNER
While making *The Magnificent Seven*, Yul Brynner approached Steve McQueen and grabbed him by the arm, saying: 'Now listen, there's a story in the paper about us having a feud. I'm an established star and I don't feud with supporting actors. I want you to call the paper and tell them the story is completely false.' McQueen refused to obey Brynner's demands and later recalled: 'He was a real uptight dude.'

LORETTA YOUNG
In 1971 Loretta Young fought one of the most curious of legal actions. She tried unsuccessfully to prevent her old films being shown on television because she believed they were damaging her image.

CLARK GABLE
Gossip columnist Sheilah Graham was banned from Clark Gable's sets for writing: 'Clark Gable threw his handsome head back and exposed a neckline on which a thin ridge of fat is beginning to collect.'

BETSY DRAKE
When Betsy Drake married Cary Grant she commented: 'I never did know how many people were present at the ceremony. I couldn't see because I didn't have my glasses on. What girl wants to be married wearing glasses?'

...And one famous director who had a weight problem

While working together on *Marnie*, Tippi Hedren and Alfred Hitchcock had a row. 'She did what no one is permitted to do. She referred to my weight,' said Hitchcock. The great director did not talk to her again during the making of the film.

Seven odd comments stars have made about their spouses

'Marriage to Monroe would be theatrically equal to five new works by Tennessee Williams.'

PLAYWRIGHT ARTHUR MILLER, MARILYN
MONROE'S THIRD HUSBAND

'The girl who had most inner sex appeal for me.'

SEAN CONNERY ON HIS FIRST WIFE, DIANE CILENTO

'This is the grandmother I sleep with. She's so Catholic she thinks Oral Roberts is a dentist and Norman Vincent Peale is a stripper.'

BOB HOPE INTRODUCING HIS WIFE, DOLORES

'I love her, not for her breasts, her buttocks or her knees but for her mind. It is inscrutable. She is like a poem.'

RICHARD BURTON ON ELIZABETH TAYLOR

'She has an incipient double chin, her legs are too short and she has a slight pot belly. She has a wonderful bosom, though.'

RICHARD BURTON ON ELIZABETH TAYLOR

'He preferred watching television than talking to me.'

BETSY DRAKE ON CARY GRANT

'I think I'm in so many of his pictures because no other actress would work with him.'

JILL IRELAND ON CHARLES BRONSON

Six stars who have said 'No'

GRETA GARBO
Garbo has persistently refused to appear on the stage unless the first fifteen rows of the theatre are left empty.

She has also refused to appear on television on the grounds that she has never watched it.

Sean Connery
Connery refused to test for the part of James Bond, telling producer Cubby Broccoli in 1961: 'You either take me as I am or not at all.'

Marlene Dietrich
In 1939 Dietrich refused an offer from Adolf Hitler to return to Germany as his mistress and the 'Queen of the Reich Cinema' and hastily completed her United States citizenship forms.

Ron Howard
The *Happy Days* star refused to renew his contract as an actor in 1980, preferring rather to direct Bette Davis in the television film *Skyward*, thereby 'fulfilling a lifetime ambition'.

Mary Pickford
The head of Paramount once offered a restless Mary Pickford $1,000 a week for five years if she promised to take a complete rest from work and agree not to make a film with another studio during that period. She refused.

Alfred Hitchcock
When the portly director was in Rome in the early 1970s his hosts arranged for him an audience with the Pope. Hitchcock refused, saying: 'What would I do if the Holy Father said that in this world, with so much sex and violence, I ought to lay off?'

... And one who was said 'no' to

George Raft
The former nightclub dancer who became Hollywood's leading sinister actor was refused entry to England in 1966 because of his alleged Mafia connections.

Seven stars who could justly boast about their fathers

Ursula Andress	Father was a German diplomat.
Brigitte Bardot	Father was a French industrialist.
Dirk Bogarde	Father was art correspondent for *The Times*.
Peter Finch	Father was an Austrian physicist.
Robert Duvall	Father was a rear admiral.
Burt Reynolds	Father was a police chief.
Paul Robeson	Father was a slave who became a Protestant minister.

... And perhaps a father in more ways than one

Walter Matthau maintains that his father was a Russian Orthodox priest.

Five stars who are unique

CARY GRANT

Cary Grant is the only film actor for whom Bloomingdales, the famous New York department store, has consented to open so that he could shop alone unmolested by crowds, at a moment when the store was shut to the general public.

CLAUDETTE COLBERT

Jack Hawkins maintained that Claudette Colbert was the only woman he didn't mind kissing on the set at an unsociable hour.

JULIE WALTERS

Julie Walters is the only actress to have been invited to appear three times in the same week on the prestigious Johnny Carson Show.

MARLENE DIETRICH
Marlene Dietrich was the only woman allowed to attend the prewar Berlin ball for male transvestites.

ELIZABETH TAYLOR
Montgomery Clift once said about his closest friend Elizabeth Taylor: 'Liz is the only woman I have ever met who turns me on. She feels like the other half of me.'

Eleven stars who are worthy of respect

INGRID BERGMAN
'She's everything a woman should be – she's the kind of woman men aren't afraid of because she's so warm. I just feel privileged to be in the same picture as her [*The Cactus Flower*].'

GOLDIE HAWN

JIMMY STEWART
'Jimmy is everything the British audience wants an American to be but so rarely is.'

SIR ANTHONY QUAYLE

MAE WEST
'I've learned everything from her. Well, not everything, but almost everything. She knows so much. Her insight is so true. Her timing so perfect, her grasp of a situation so right.'

CARY GRANT

CLARK GABLE
'Oh, Gable has enemies all right – but they all like him.'

DAVID SELZNICK

LAUREN BACALL
'One of the smartest of all Hollywood's tempting women.

49

'"Betty" never flaunts her loveliness, nor her intellect. A man in her presence is only conscious of her charm.'

JOHN WAYNE

ALAN LADD
'That man had stature even if he was short.'

STEWART GRANGER

SALLY FIELD
'She's tough, she's gritty, she's got a great sense of humour and she gets prettier every day.'

BURT REYNOLDS

CARY GRANT
'I think that anyone who really knows this man – really knows him – loves him. You can't help it.'

DYAN CANNON

DEBORAH KERR
'She is the only star I know who genuinely treats each and everybody exactly alike.'

JULIA FOSTER

BOB HOPE
'There is a man.'

JOHN STEINBECK

JULIE ANDREWS
'The last of the truly great dames.'

PAUL NEWMAN

Five witty replies from Marilyn Monroe

Q: 'Is it true you wear falsies?'
A: 'Those who know me better know better.'

Q: 'Did you have anything on?'
A: 'Oh yes, I had the radio on.'
   (When it was discovered that she had posed nude for a calendar.)

Q: 'Is it true you are having trouble with the Johnston office?'
A: 'Their trouble is that they worry whether a girl has cleavage. They ought to worry if she hasn't any.'

Q: 'Miss Monroe, what are your feelings about sex?'
A: 'Sex is part of nature and I go along with nature.'

Q: 'Miss Monroe, what do you wear at night?'
A: 'Chanel No. 5.'

Six strange coincidences

CASABLANCA
Casablanca, which was made without prior knowledge of the American landings in North Africa, was released just a week after the landings took place in Casablanca itself in 1942.

PC 007
The screen's most famous James Bond, Sean Connery, was once served a speeding summons by a Sergeant James Bond. After giving evidence Sergeant Bond told the press: 'I feel I'm unfortunate to have been born with the name but there's nothing I can do about it.'

CALL OF GOD
Tyrone Power died on the set of *The Miracle Man* in 1931. His more famous son, Tyrone Power Junior, died while filming *Solomon and Sheba* in 1958.

ONLY THE BEST WILL DO
It's a strange coincidence that Warren Beatty's three greatest loves, Leslie Caron (*The L-shaped Room*), Julie Christie (*Darling*) and Diane Keaton (*Annie Hall*) started going out with him after they had either just been nominated or had just won an Academy Award.

RESEARCHING THE ROLE
Indian superstar Uptal Dutt was arrested as a political agitator only weeks before filming was due to commence on *The Agitator*. Yves Montand and Marilyn Monroe also took things a little too literally when they admitted to an affair while filming *Let's Make Love*. Janet Leigh wasn't quite so thorough, for although she had been a student of Psychology it didn't stop her getting murdered in a shower in *Psycho*.

ESP
Shirley Maclaine was entertaining some friends in an apartment in Malibu, Florida, when she suddenly screamed: 'Peter, something has happened to Peter Sellers.' A few minutes later the phone rang. It was a reporter asking her to comment on Peter Sellers' death.

Twelve personal insults

'She was venomous, vicious, a pathological liar, and quite stupid.'

RAY MILLAND ON HEDDA HOPPER

'The only Greek tragedy I know.'

BILLY WILDER ON SPYROS SKOURAS

'His popularity within the industry is not legendary.'

DAVID SHIPMAN ON CHARLES BRONSON

'I've seen him turn into this arrogant, sour, ceremonial, pious, chauvinistic egomaniac.'

ELLIOT GOULD ON JERRY LEWIS

'A face unclouded by thought.'

LILLIAN HELLMAN ON NORMA SHEARER

'So many people came to his funeral because they wanted to make sure the S.O.B. was dead.'

SAMUEL GOLDWYN ON LOUIS MAYER

'A grubby cherub.'

JONATHAN MILLER ON DUDLEY MOORE

'He recognized no authority, no discipline, no frontiers except his own gigantic appetite for food, drink and women.'

HEDDA HOPPER ON MARIO LANZA

'Susannah was the personification of uninformed arrogance of youth.'

JOHN HUSTON ON SUSANNAH YORK

'He has the memory of an elephant and the hide of an elephant. The only difference is that elephants are vegetarians and Mayer's diet is his fellow man.'

HERMAN MANKIEWICZ ON LOUIS MAYER

'The most pretentious woman the cinema has ever known.'

RYAN O'NEAL ON BARBRA STREISAND

'The Robert Stigwood organization is to the cinema what Macdonalds is to cuisine.'

DAVID SHIPMAN ON ROBERT STIGWOOD

Nine films that got it wrong

The Viking Queen
Set in the times of Boudicca, a wristwatch is clearly visible on one of the leading characters.

One Million Years B C
All the girls wear false eyelashes.

The Wrong Box
The roofs of Victorian London are littered with TV aerials.

Psycho
If you look closely at Janet Leigh as she lies 'dead', you will see her gulp twice.

Scipio Africanus
This awful film is only worth watching for the fact that the cast wear wristwatches with their togas and that during the Battle of Zama you can see telegraph poles in the background.

Emma Hamilton
This film is set in 1804 and Big Ben manages to strike, although it wasn't built for another fifty years.

Triple Cross
A Second World War film which has a newspaper headline about the soaring cost of Concorde.

Carmen Jones
The camera tracks Dorothy Dandridge down a street and the entire film crew is reflected in a shop window.

Decameron Nights
Louis Jourdan stands on the deck of his fourteenth-century pirate ship and a white lorry trundles down the hill in the background.

Ten subjects Marlene Dietrich refused to discuss

At the height of her fame, Marlene Dietrich instructed Paramount officials to inform the press that the following subjects bored her and therefore she refused to discuss them:

Horse-racing
Evangelism
Fish
Radio
Police dogs
After-dinner speeches
Dieting
Sopranos
First nights
Slang

Eight precocious stars

ZSA ZSA GABOR
Zsa Zsa Gabor was voted Miss Hungary at the age of fifteen, and just a year later she was married and a society hostess.

BROOKE SHIELDS AND JODIE FOSTER
Brooke Shields played a child prostitute in *Pretty Baby* when she was only fourteen, but she was still older than Jodie Foster who was thirteen when she played a similar role in *Taxi Driver*.

SHIRLEY TEMPLE
Shirley Temple starred in over twenty films from 1934 to 1938. She received a special Academy Award 'in grateful recognition of her outstanding contribution to screen entertainment during

the year 1934' at the age of seven. She married, relatively late considering, aged seventeen.

JEAN HARLOW, SHEREE NORTH AND JUNE HAVOC

Jean Harlow was married at the age of sixteen and Sheree North became a wife when she was only fifteen. But they are both overshadowed by June Havoc, who was married at twelve.

CHARLES BRONSON

In a rare interview, Charles Bronson told *Esquire* magazine that he made love at the age of five and a half (to a six-year-old girl) and at the same age he started chewing tobacco. He began smoking at the mature age of nine.

The seven deadly whims

In *Prodigal Daughters* (1923), Gloria Swanson proclaimed the seven deadly whims:

New lips to kiss
Freedom from convention
A new world for women
No more chaperons
Life with a kick in it
The single moral standard
Our own latchkeys

Ten memorable lines

'Hello there, warm, dark and handsome.'
MAE WEST to CARY GRANT in *She Done Him Wrong*

'I think you're the most attractive of all my parents' friends.'

> BENJAMIN BRADDOCK (DUSTIN HOFFMAN) to MRS
> ROBINSON (ANNE BANCROFT) in *The Graduate*

'If you want me just whistle...'

> LAUREN BACALL in *To Have and Have Not*

'I'm still big, it's the pictures that got small.'

> GLORIA SWANSON (NORMA DESMOND) in *Sunset Boulevard*

'Suckers.'

> MAE WEST in *I'm No Angel*

'Back to the cage, Freeson.'

> PAUL FORD in *A Big Hand for the Little Lady*

'You ain't heard nothin' yet.'

> AL JOLSON in *The Jazz Singer*

'I know – a man's gotta do what a man's gotta do.'

> LEE J. COBB to CLINT EASTWOOD in *Coogan's Bluff*

'I'm a man who likes to talk to a man who likes to talk.'

> SYDNEY GREENSTREET to HUMPHREY BOGART in
> *The Maltese Falcon*

'I'd like a cigarette.'

> Memorable for being the last line of *Heaven's Gate*

Ten lines we would rather have not heard

'Fish, I love you and I respect you very much.'

> SPENCER TRACY in *The Old Man and the Sea*

'You are a thirsty plant, Pamela – Giorgio can water you.'

> LUCIANO PAVAROTTI (GIORGIO) to his mistress in
> *Yes Giorgio*

Jesus Christ: 'What is your name, my friend?'
James the Younger: 'James, little James. They call me little because I'm the youngest. What is yours?'

Jesus Christ: 'Jesus.'
James the Younger: 'Ah, that's a good name.'
Jesus Christ: 'Thank you.'

From The Greatest Story Ever Told

'You know, you're more beautiful than any girl I know.'

BO DEREK (JANE) to (MILES O'KEEFE) TARZAN in
Tarzan the Ape Man

'Kind of shame kids have to grow up to be people.'

JOHN WAYNE (DAVY CROCKETT) to RICHARD
WIDMARK in The Alamo

'Where's the rest of me?'

RONALD REAGAN, having just woken up to find one of his
legs amputated, in King's Row

... And perhaps the best remembered line, for all the wrong reasons, in the history of the cinema

'Truly this man was the Son of God.'

JOHN WAYNE as the centurion at the foot of the cross, in
The Greatest Story Ever Told

Seven early cinema captions

'No smoking please. It annoys the ladies.'

'Please read the titles to yourself. Loud reading annoys your neighbours.'

'Just a moment ... please ... while the operator changes the reel.'

'Ladies kindly remove your hats.'

'Ladies and children are cordially invited to this theatre. No offensive pictures are ever shown here.'

If annoyed when here – please tell the management.'

'Our patrons are our friends.'

Six of the funniest lines in films

'I never remember a face.'
>SHIRLEY MACLAINE playing a prostitute in *Irma La Douce*

'What am I saying?'
>ERROL FLYNN in *Northern Pursuit* after telling the heroine that she was the only girl he had ever loved. At the time of filming, he was involved in a rape case.

'Alligators have the right idea – they eat their young.'
>EVE ARDEN to JOAN CRAWFORD in *Mildred Pierce*

'Your advertising's great. People'd never guess you got nothing to sell.'
>BONNIE (FAYE DUNAWAY) on CLYDE'S (WARREN BEATTY) impotence in *Bonnie and Clyde*

'I could dance with you till the cows come home. On second thoughts I'd rather dance with the cows till you come home.'
>GROUCHO MARX in *Duck Soup*

'Ah don't sleep with whores – at least not knowingly.'
>MOLLY (WALTER MATTHAU), the HITMAN, in *Charlie Varrick*

... And one witty reply

Mrs Teasdale: 'As chairwoman of the reception committee, I welcome you with open arms.'

Rufus T. Firefly: 'Is that so? How long do you stay open?'
GROUCHO MARX as RUFUS T. FIREFLY, MARGARET
DUMONT as MRS TEASDALE, in *The Marx Brothers
at the Circus*

Two women who were surprised at the cinema

THE NAKED USHERETTE
During a screening of *The Exorcist* at La Pampa Cinema, Rio de
Janeiro, in 1974, the audience was distracted by an usherette
scampering backwards and forwards across the screen pur-
suing a rat with a mop. To cries of 'Get them off', she started to
disrobe. It was while dancing naked in front of the screen that
she noticed the auditorium being cleared by armed police.
Explaining her behaviour the usherette said later: 'I thought
the audience was calling for me. I was as surprised as anyone.'

THE HYSTERICAL FILMGOER
Midway through the screening of the première of *Heaven's Gate*
at Grauman's Chinese Theatre, an hysterical fan ran out of the
theatre and shouted to a man pacing up and down in the lobby:
'This is the most disgusting, degrading and horrible film I've
ever seen.' Little did she know that the man to whom she had
addressed these comments was Michael Cimino, the director
of *Heaven's Gate*.

...And one man who was embarrassed at the cinema

At a sneak preview of *That Hagen Girl* there was a loud chorus of
'Oh no!' when Ronald Reagan said to Shirley Temple: 'I love
you, will you marry me?' Reagan recalls that he shrank down
in his seat after the audience's reaction and refused to leave the
cinema until everybody else had gone. The line was later cut
from the film.

Ten more notable firsts

Elizabeth Taylor was the first Hollywood star to receive one million dollars for a single film – the film being the disastrous *Cleopatra* in 1963.

The first person to appear naked on the screen was Hedy Lamarr.

The first all-negro film was *Darktown Justice* in 1914.

The word 'Bugger' was first allowed in *Who's afraid of Virginia Woolf* in 1966. 'Fuck' was first uttered by Marianne Faithful in *I'll Never Forget Whatsisname* in 1966.

The first movie fight was between Tom Farnum and Tom Santschi in the 1914 version of Rex Beach's *The Spoilers*.

The first words Greta Garbo spoke on the screen were: 'Gif me a viskey, ginger ale on the side – and don't be stingy, Baby,' in *Anna Christie*.

The first X certificate was given to *Birds in Peru*, a story of nymphomania.

The Outlaw (1941) was the first American film to suggest homosexuality might be enjoyable.

The first film with a story was *The Great Train Robbery* in 1903.

Sir Alec Guinness was the first British actor to become a dollar millionaire for his role in *Star Wars*. He was on $2\frac{1}{2}$ per cent of the film's gross takings.

Ten famous prostitutes

Diane Cilento	*Rattle of a Simple Man.*
Bette Davis	*Of Human Bondage.*

Marlene Dietrich	*Dishonoured.*
Catherine Deneuve	*Belle de Jour.*
Jane Fonda	*Klute.*
Greta Garbo	*Anna Christie.*
Margot Kidder	*Gaily, Gaily.*
Sophia Loren	*Man of La Mancha.*
Shirley Maclaine	*Irma La Douce.*
Elizabeth Taylor	*Butterfield 8.*

Ten love affairs between the stars that needed no direction

Richard Burton – Elizabeth Taylor	*Cleopatra.*
Clint Eastwood – Sondra Locke	*Every Which Way but Loose.*
Peter Finch – Vivien Leigh	*Elephant Walk.*
Robert Donat – Madeleine Carroll	*The 39 Steps.*
Steve McQueen – Ali McGraw	*The Getaway.*
Warren Beatty – Natalie Wood	*Splendour in the Grass.*
William Powell – Jean Harlow	*Reckless.*
Stewart Granger – Deborah Kerr	*Caesar and Cleopatra.*
Sidney Poitier – Joanna Shimkus	*The Lost Man.*
Al Pacino – Marthe Keller	*Bobby Deerfield.*

Seven lines immortalized by Mae West

'Come up and see me sometime.'

'You can be had.'

'Beulah, peel me a grape.'

'It's not the men in my life that counts – it's the life in my men.'

'I collect diamonds – it's m'hobby.'

'Goodness, what lovely diamonds.'
'Goodness has nothing to do with it.'

'Give me a sixteen-year-old and I'll return him at twenty-one.'

Three stars who have been answered back

ORSON WELLES
While making *The Lady From Shanghai*, Orson Welles had a running feud with the production manager, Jack Fier. It came to the point where Welles posted a sign reading:
    'We have nothing to fear but Fier himself.'
    Fier replied with a sign which read:
    'All's well that ends Welles.'

OLIVER REED
Oliver Reed lost a golf club while playing the seventh hole at Sandy Lane, Barbados. When asked about the missing club, his caddie protested:
    'I'm paid to watch de ball, man, not de club.'

LORD OLIVIER
When Lord Olivier was making *The Prince and the Pauper*, he shouted at his leading lady, Marilyn Monroe:
    'Why can't you get here on time, for fuck's sake?'
    'Oh, do you have that word in England, too?' she replied.

... And one who would have liked to

JEANNE MOREAU
'Before he [Burt Lancaster] can pick up an ashtray, he

discusses his motivation for an hour or two. You want to say: "Just pick up the ashtray and shut up."''

Eleven stars who have enjoyed blowing their own trumpets

GABRIELLINO D'ANNUNZIO
The Italian director of *Quo Vadis*, nicknamed 'the John the Baptist of Fascism', used to boast publicly that he drank wine from the skull of a virgin who had committed suicide for his sake.

CECIL B. DE MILLE
The famous film director boasted in 1924 that: 'I have brought a certain sense of beauty and luxury into everyday existence.'

POLA NEGRI
'Hollywood has gone from Pola to Polaroid,' commented actress Pola Negri on her retirement in the mid-1960s.

DOUGLAS FAIRBANKS
The great swashbuckler was once asked to list his hobbies on a form. He simply wrote: 'Doug.'

DARRYL F. ZANUCK
When he was head of production at Warner Brothers, he used to inform young actresses that: 'You've had nothing until you've had me! I am the biggest and the best! I can go on all night and all day.'

WALTER MATTHAU
In *Pete 'n' Tillie*, Walter Matthau takes his girlfriend to a cinema showing *Lonely Are the Brave*, one of his earlier films.

NOEL COWARD

'The two most beautiful things in the world,' Coward once said, 'are Ivor Novello's profile and my mind.'

GINA LOLLOBRIGIDA

The Italian temptress maintains that she had a tough time at art school because she was kept from her easel by constant demands from the other students to pose for them.

WARREN BEATTY

When Warren Beatty was offered the role of John F. Kennedy in *PT 109*, studio boss Jack Warner suggested to him that he should go to Washington and study the President's mannerisms. Beatty was unimpressed. 'If the President wants me to play him,' he replied, 'tell him to come here and soak up my atmosphere.'

CHARLES BRONSON

'Us legends,' Charles Bronson once said, 'tend to get picky in our twilight years.'

RICHARD BURTON

When Richard Burton and Elizabeth Taylor were married and for some reason or other Burton was not at home, the Welshman used to boast that his wife went to bed with his socks instead.

Princess Diana's supporting cast

Humphrey Bogart	Seventh cousin twice removed.
Orson Welles	Eighth cousin twice removed.
Lillian Gish	Double seventh cousin three times removed.
Lee Remick	Tenth cousin.
Olivia de Havilland	Fifth cousin three times removed.

Seven films that received terrible reviews

Mr Parkinson
'It's two hours too long.'
  (The film lasts 121 mins.)   Anon.

Sincerely Yours
'Given sufficient intoxication you could find this movie amusing.'
                                The Saturday Review

Can't Stop The Music
'Some scenes could pulp and solve the paper shortage, they are so wooden.'
                                         Variety

At Long Last Love
'If this film were any more of a dog, it would shed.'
                                    John Barbour

Bride of Vengeance
'A dud ... it just couldn't be this bad by accident.'   Anon.

Miss Lulu Bett
'No one likes this film but the public.'
                                 William C. De Mille

The Deerhunter
'A travesty of the war and an insult to those who fought in it.'
                                    The Spectator

... And one very odd piece of casting

On the casting of John Wayne as Genghis Khan in *The Conqueror*:

'History's most improbable piece of casting, unless Mickey Rooney were to play Jesus Christ in *The King of Kings*.'

Jack Smith, *Los Angeles Times*

Five people who were wrong

JACK WARNER
Irving Asher screentested Merle Oberon and sent the test to Jack Warner, who replied by telegram: 'If you want to sleep with women go ahead, but don't waste my money testing them.'

JULIE CHRISTIE
Julie Christie said of her boyfriend Don Bessant in 1966: 'I don't imagine I'll ever want anyone but Don.' They broke up the following year.

LARRY 'BUSTER' CRABBE
On being told the plot for *Flash Gordon* (1936) the star Larry 'Buster' Crabbe said: 'They're goddam nuts!' Universal, as it happens, were quite right – it was their second biggest money maker of the year.

MRS WALTERS
Julie Walters' mother told her daughter that if she became an actress she would be in the gutter by the time she was twenty.

MARLON BRANDO
Brando married Anna Kashfi in 1957 believing that she was pure Indian, but he soon left her when he discovered that she was pure Welsh. They were divorced in 1959.

Five offers that were rejected

The part of 'Alfie' (1966) was turned down by Anthony Newley, James Booth and Laurence Harvey before Michael Caine accepted the role and the subsequent road to stardom.

Five actors were offered the male lead in *Love Story* – Beau Bridges, Jon Voight, Michael Sarrazin, Michael York and Michael Douglas – before Ryan O'Neal eventually took the part.

Former US Secretary of State Henry Kissinger offered to fly to Texas and negotiate personally with Ali McGraw on her husband Robert Evans' behalf, when he heard the news that she was having an affair with Steve McQueen.

Warren Beatty, Robert Redford, Steve McQueen, Paul Newman and James Caan all turned down the role of 'Superman'. It was eventually snapped up by Christopher Reeve.

Frankie Howerd was turned down for *Stars in Battledress*. He auditioned four times but was unsuccessful; consequently he had to take an acting active part in the D-Day Landings. His commanding officer told him: 'You are being posted to Plymouth for the big show – and I don't mean telling jokes, what?'

Four stars who have suffered nervous breakdowns

PETER FINCH
In 1961 Peter Finch had a breakdown after reading of the death of television personality Gilbert Harding. Finch had idolized Errol Flynn and Gilbert Harding, referring to them as 'Up Yours Men'. The close proximity of their deaths combined with his own personal problems proved too much to handle.

GENE TIERNEY

In 1955 Gene Tierney entered the Menninger Clinic in Idaho after her first child Daria was born retarded due to Tierney having contracted German Measles during her pregnancy.

ROBERT WALKER

After having been convicted for drunken driving and divorced by Jennifer Jones, Robert Walker spent a long period of time in a mental clinic. In 1951 he returned to the screen triumphantly in *Strangers on a Train*.

SHELLEY WINTERS

After discovering that the wife of her lover, Burt Lancaster, was expecting a child Shelley Winters had a nervous breakdown.

Seven Americans who could be accused of having gone over the top

RICHARD SCHICKEL

The *Time* magazine journalist once wrote about Woody Allen that he was 'Somebody who belongs on anyone's shortlist of today's essential cultural Clarifiers and Consolations'.

PRESIDENT F. D. ROOSEVELT

In the mid-1930s King George VI and Queen Elizabeth visited America. President Roosevelt introduced them to the expansive singer Kate Smith saying: 'This is Kate Smith, this is America.'

BOB HOPE

The British-born comedian once said of Jack Benny: 'Jack had that rare magic – that indefinable something called genius. Picasso had it, Gershwin had it, and Jack was blessed by it. He didn't just stand on the stage ... he owned it.'

A *TIME* MAGAZINE JOURNALIST

The journalist wrote about Julie Andrews: 'She is Christmas Carols in the snow, a companion by the fire, a laughing clown at charades, a girl to read poetry to on a cold winter's night.' (Quite what his reaction was when she went topless in *S.O.B.* we do not know.)

PRESIDENT R. NIXON

The President said of Bob Hope in 1970 that: 'America owes a great deal to Britain ... our common law... our language... and many of our political institutions ... But we are particularly indebted to England for giving us Bob Hope.'

YET ANOTHER *TIME* MAGAZINE JOURNALIST

In 1962 a journalist wrote of Sophia Loren: 'She has rewritten the canons of beauty. A daughter of the Bay of Naples, she has within her blood of the Saracens, Spaniards, Normans, Byzantines and Greeks. The East appears in her slanting eyes, her dark brown hair is a bazaar of rare silk ...'

PRESIDENT J. F. KENNEDY

Three months before her death, Marilyn Monroe sang 'Happy Birthday' to President Kennedy at a party in New York. The President commented afterwards: 'I can now retire from politics after having Happy Birthday sung to me by Miss Monroe.'

Five author actors

DIANE CILENTO

The first wife of Sean Connery has written, among other novels, *The Manipulator*.

TONY CURTIS
Roger Moore's partner in TV's *The Persuaders* wrote a novel called *Kid Cody and Julie Sparrow*.

HERBERT LOM
The neurotic inspector of *Pink Panther* fame wrote a book about the playwright Philip Marlowe entitled *Enter the Spy*.

ROBERT SHAW
The star who played Henry VIII in *A Man for All Seasons* wrote a number of novels including *The Hiding Place* and *The Man in the Glass Booth*. The latter was adapted for the stage and was a hit on both Broadway and the West End.

RUDOLPH VALENTINO
Valentino and his wife Natacha Rambova wrote a book of verse called *Daydreams*.

Three successful predictions

'He never really felt like an actor at all, his real interest might lie in public service of another kind. Perhaps politics . . .'
Film MAGAZINE ON RONALD REAGAN, 1947

'Alan Bennett, Jonathan Miller, Peter Cook and Dudley Moore. Remember these names. You'll hear them again.'
MAURICE CHEVALIER, 1962

'This boy is a genius and will be a great actor. He is outstandingly handsome and robust, very muscular and has a deep inward fire.'
NEVILLE COGHILL, OXFORD UNIVERSITY
TUTOR TO RICHARD BURTON

The religious beliefs of five stars

PETER O'TOOLE
The Irish half-reformed hell-raiser has described himself as a 'retired Christian'.

VIVIEN LEIGH
The convent-educated *Gone with the Wind* star described herself, late in life, as a 'Zen-Buddhist-Catholic'.

JAMES FOX
The Englishman best known for his performance in Losey's *The Servant* abandoned acting in the 1970s for eight years to become an Evangelist.

LEW AYRES
The star of *All Quiet on the Western Front*, who was once married to Ginger Rogers, now devotes his time to the study of philosophy and comparative religion.

SPENCER TRACY
The great man's Catholic beliefs prevented him from divorcing his wife, Louise Treadwell, though they didn't appear to prevent him having much publicized liaisons with Loretta Young and Katharine Hepburn.

Five phobias of the stars

Hydrophobia	Burt Lancaster.
The size of her bottom	Grace Kelly.
Claustrophobia	Charles Bronson.

Insomnia	Peter O'Toole (considers himself lucky if he sleeps for an hour at night).
The size of her feet	Greta Garbo.

Five stars comment on money

'If someone was stupid enough to offer me a million dollars to make a picture, I was certainly not dumb enough to turn it down.'

ELIZABETH TAYLOR

'I just take the money and use it on things which really interest me.'

GEORGE SANDERS

'Just enough to be able to say No.'

KATHARINE HEPBURN

'I'm not rich, but I don't need money as much as I used to, so I no longer need to make crap.'

BETTE DAVIS

'Nothing is beneath me if it pays well. I've earned the right to damn well grab whatever I can in the time I've got left.'

LORD OLIVIER, 1982

Four actors who could safely be taken home to meet their girlfriends' mothers

PETER FINCH
'Everybody adored Peter so much that he would just come on to the set and everyone would start smiling.'

VIRGINIA MCKENNA

RAY MILLAND
'This enormously famous star is so self-effacingly modest, he's an object lesson for the rest of us in show business.'
FRANKIE HOWERD

NOEL COWARD
'. . . if and when I finally do it, I kill my mother-in-law or I rape a nun, and I'm in the cooler for ever. When everybody else sees fit to disown me Noel will come and see me every day.'
DAVID NIVEN

JACK BUCHANAN
'You never heard stories against Jack because there simply weren't stories to tell. He wasn't a subject for muck-raking because there wasn't any muck.'
WILFRED HYDE-WHITE

Six unlikely passions of the stars

Nuts	Richard Burton.
Passion for cleaning the houses of her friends	Marlene Dietrich.
Magic and magicians	Cary Grant.
Personal hygiene (he used to take four showers a day)	William Holden.
Poker	Sophia Loren.
Playing the piano	Jimmy Stewart.

Seven inauspicious débuts

A LABORATORY ASSISTANT
In 1955 Clint Eastwood, with the help of a rat in his pocket, played the part of a laboratory assistant in the three-dimensional film *Revenge of the Creature from the Black Lagoon*.

A NUBILE MAJORETTE
At the age of twenty-two, Boston-born actress Lee Remick played a drum majorette in the 1957 film *A Face in the Crowd*.

A JUGGLER
The Polish-born actress Nastassia Kinski made her début in 1975 as a juggler in *The Wrong Movement*.

A DRUG-SMUGGLER
Yul 'Just call me a nice, clean-cut Mongolian boy' Brynner played the part of a particularly unpleasant drug-smuggler in *The Port of New York* in 1949, when he was thirty-four.

A SLAVE
Italian screen goddess Sophia Loren can be spotted by the eagle-eyed cinema-goer as one of ten thousand slave girls in the 1951 version of *Quo Vadis?*

A PUPPET'S GIRLFRIEND
American comedienne Carol Burnett's first public performance was on a television show playing the part of a ventriloquist's dummy's girlfriend.

OBSCENE SINGER
In 1900 Maurice Chevalier made his professional début, aged twelve, singing obscene songs to French café audiences of pimps and prostitutes.

Eight honest remarks

'I guess I look like a rock quarry that someone has dynamited.'
CHARLES BRONSON

'I've never done a film I'm proud of.'
STEWART GRANGER, 1968

'I guess I'm happiest when I'm looking reasonably like a slob.'
SHIRLEY MACLAINE

'I worked like a son of a bitch to learn a few tricks and I fight like a steer to avoid getting stuck with parts I can't play.'
CLARK GABLE

'If I'd had a face like Elizabeth Taylor's I would never have won my two Oscars.'
BETTE DAVIS

'I simply didn't feel qualified to put words into the mouth of one whom hundreds of millions devoutly believe to be their saviour.'
Philip Dunne, explaining why he turned down the opportunity to write and direct *The Greatest Story Ever Told*

'I can't say the mini made me an actress but it sure helped make me a star.'
RAQUEL WELCH

'I talk on and on to obtain an approximation of what I mean. As for being an ad lib wit . . . never!'
FRANKIE HOWERD

Ten native New Yorkers

Lauren Bacall
James Caan
Tony Curtis

76

Robert De Niro
Kirk Douglas
Jane Fonda
Burt Lancaster
Lee Marvin
Walter Matthau
Sylvester Stallone

Two stars who have been reduced to tears

KIRK DOUGLAS
Once when Burt Lancaster and Kirk Douglas were walking off the set after completing a scene of *Gunfight at the OK Corral* a crowd of autograph hunters surrounded Burt Lancaster. 'Why don't you ask Mr Douglas for his?' he asked, and then added: 'Great performer. Of course you don't recognize him without his built-up shoes.' Moments later Kirk Douglas started to cry.

SHIRLEY TEMPLE
In all Shirley Temple's films her tears were real. She would be told that she couldn't have lunch that day and would start to cry. To get her to stop they would bring her something to eat. When she became older the director would tell her that she wasn't going to ever see her mother again, that she had gone away and was never coming back. Shirley would then start to cry.

The last screen appearance of ten stars

Gary Cooper	*The Naked Edge.*
Clark Gable	*The Misfits*
Betty Grable	*How To Be Very Very Popular.*

Boris Karloff	*The House of Evil.*
Carole Lombard	*To Be Or Not To Be.*
Jayne Mansfield	*A Guide For The Married Man.*
The Marx Brothers	*Love Happy.*
Marilyn Monroe	*The Misfits.*
Sir Ralph Richardson	*Give My Regards To Broad Street.*
John Wayne	*The Shootist.*

Seven comments on the art of acting

'I'm not ashamed of the Bond films. Quality is not only to be found at the Old Vic, and portraying Bond is just as serious as playing Macbeth.'

SEAN CONNERY

'Dramatic art in her opinion is knowing how to fill a sweater.'

BETTE DAVIS ON JAYNE MANSFIELD

'Acting is the easiest thing I've ever done – I guess that's why I stick with it. I'm just a bum at heart.'

CHARLES BRONSON

'Left eyebrow raised, right eyebrow raised.'

ROGER MOORE ON HIS ACTING RANGE

Film producer: 'In *Superman II* you look so cruel and evil yet you really seem to be such fun. How do you manage it?'
Sarah Douglas: 'In England, dear, we call it acting.'

'His performance drunk or sober was the way other actors tend to perform if drunk.'

OSCAR MILLAND, SCREENWRITER OF *The Conqueror*, ON JOHN WAYNE

'What I do try to do is to give the impression of being spontaneous. It's acting, and if I can claim to be an actor at all that is what I do with it.'

FRANKIE HOWERD

Six people who became stars despite physical imperfections

HUMPHREY BOGART
Bogart's lisp was caused by a badly performed operation on his lower lip in which a splinter of wood had become embedded.

STACY KEACH
TV's 'Mike Hammer' has a scarred mouth because of four operations to remove a hare-lip.

HERBERT MARSHALL
Though this British actor lost a leg in the First World War he still enjoyed a successful Hollywood career playing gentlemanly roles.

LIONEL BARRYMORE
From 1938, crippled by arthritis and having twice broken his hip, Lionel Barrymore continued his acting career from a wheelchair.

SUSAN PETERS
This American leading lady of the Forties was badly injured in a car crash but continued to act from a wheelchair until her early death in 1952 aged thirty-one.

CARY GRANT
This Bristol-born 'smoothie', whom many consider the most handsome leading man of them all, is at least not quite perfect

because owing to a playground accident he has only one large upper front tooth in the centre of his mouth.

Five deaths shrouded in mystery

LINDA DARNELL
In 1965 aged forty-one Linda Darnell was found dead in a friend's sitting room. She had apparently lit a cigarette which set fire to the room. At the time she was beset with emotional and weight problems.

HARRY BAUR
This celebrated French actor was arrested in 1942 by the Gestapo for forging papers to prove his Aryan origins in order to fool the German authorities into allowing him to star in a two million mark production. He was tortured and eventually released in 1943. He died mysteriously two days later.

NATALIE WOOD
The former child actress died mysteriously in 1981 at the age of forty-three. She reputedly left her husband, Robert Wagner, and co-star Christopher Walken quarrelling on a yacht. She was found a few hours later, drowned, with a high blood alcohol level.

LESLIE HOWARD
This popular Englishman was killed in 1943 at the age of fifty flying back to London after a secret wartime mission to Lisbon. Many believe that Howard had been used as a decoy to divert attention from Churchill, who was also flying that day.

SAL MINEO
The diminutive actor who starred with James Dean in *Giant* and *Rebel Without a Cause* was stabbed in the chest outside his

West Hollywood apartment on 12 February 1976. No motive
has ever been discovered.

Four cases of censorship

THE MEANING OF THE WORD 'SHEIK'
Senator Henry L. Meyers put in the Congressional Record in
June 1922 a statement to enforce censorship of the movies
immediately. He was particularly concerned about Rudolph
Valentino and the interpretation of the word 'sheik'.

TOO REALISTIC
When Sir John Mills's love scene with Sylvia Sims in *Ice Cold in
Alex* was censored the distinguished actor was unrepentant.
'It's a sheer relief to play a real love scene with a girl for a
change, after so many years of giving them polite pecks on the
cheek between battles.'

NOT FOR ROYAL EARS
Only hours before the Royal Première of *The Wicked Lady* in
1945 two ladies-in-waiting announced after seeing the film that
some of its language was unsuitable for Royal ears. It was
eventually agreed that some of the dialogue should be rendered
inaudible.

GROPING HAND
Although Rock Hudson and Doris Day were playing a married
couple they were put in separate bath tubs for a scene in *Pillow
Talk* (1959) but can be seen on both sides of a split screen. The
censor cut the sequence in the film where Doris Day loses her
soap and puts her hand through the screen, into her co-star's
tub.

Six stars over six feet tall

John Wayne	6′ 4″
Rock Hudson	6′ 4″
Clint Eastwood	6′ 4″
James Stewart	6′ 3″
Charlton Heston	6′ 3″
Warren Beatty	6′ 1″

Five cases of extreme bad luck

THE BRITISH IMPRESARIO

Sir Lew Grade, after a series of box office flops including *Escape To Athena*, *Movie Movie* and *Raise the Titanic*, was eased out of his own production company. Unfortunately for Sir Lew the very same year they had a major success – *On Golden Pond*.

THE POLE AND THE COCKTAIL

Vladek Sheybal, Polish character actor (*Women In Love*), was caught carrying Molotov cocktails through the German lines during the Warsaw Rising. He was sent to a concentration camp.

THE LAW AND FOUR MILLION DOLLARS

Jackie Coogan was twenty-one in 1935. He therefore asked his mother for the four million dollars he had earned as a child star. He was surprised when his mother asserted that she had discovered a Californian law which stated that the earnings of a minor are the absolute property of his parents. Coogan was refused any money by his mother.

TWO STARS AND A LACK OF FESTIVE SPIRIT

Humphrey Bogart was born on Christmas Day (1899), which he deeply resented. He once commented: 'Got gypped out of a proper birthday, goddamit.' W.C.Fields died on Christmas Day (1946) – a festival which above all he loathed.

... And one case of extreme bravery

PATRICIA NEAL
At the height of her fame, the actress who won an Oscar for her performance in *Hud* was the victim of a tragic sequence of events. Firstly, her young daughter died from measles, then her baby son was gravely injured in a road accident, and finally she suffered from a severe stroke that left her paralysed. Her heroic recovery inspired a television film, *The Patricia Neal Story* (1981).

The vital statistics of five stars

Jayne Mansfield	$40 - 18\frac{1}{2} - 36$
Anita Ekberg	$39 - 23 - 37$
Joan Collins	$38 - 23\frac{1}{2} - 37$
Sophia Loren	$38 - 24 - 38$

('It's like being bombed by watermelons', said Alan Ladd when working with Sophia on *Boy On A Dolphin*.)

Gina Lollobrigida	$36 - 22 - 35$

('Sophia's may be bigger, but not better.')

Five stars who liked a drink

ROBERT MITCHUM
In 1962 Robert Mitchum was filming *Rampage* in Hawaii when he discovered a cocktail made from pineapple juice and seven different types of rum called a 'Maitai'. He would have seven of

these as an aperitif before dinner, which works out at about forty-nine measures of rum.

RICHARD HARRIS
On the set of *The Long and The Short and the Tall* (1961), lots would be drawn amongst the younger crew members to see who would be chosen to nip across to the pub to request Richard Harris's presence back on the set. On one occasion a patrol returned from the pub after an hour, bearing the body of a completely unconscious young crew member.

FRANK SINATRA
During the filming of *From Here to Eternity* (1953) Burt Lancaster spent so much time carrying an inebriated Frank Sinatra to bed and undressing him that to this day Sinatra calls him 'Mom'. 'He'll find me on my birthday no matter where I am, and say: "Happy Birthday Mom",' says Lancaster.

PETER O'TOOLE
Monday morning shooting schedules on the set of *Country Dance* (1970) left out Peter O'Toole because it was taken for granted that he would not have returned from the drinking session he had started the previous Friday night. O'Toole once said: 'Drink is like death. You don't mind the dying, you just can't stand the pain.'

ROBERT NEWTON
Treasure Island star Robert Newton once went to sleep when he was acting in a film, in the dress circle of a theatre. The director, aware of his star's drinking habits, decided to let him sleep it off, and transferred the rest of the cast and the film crew to the stalls to shoot another scene. When Newton eventually woke up, not realizing where everybody was, he relieved himself over the balcony.

... And one who felt he needed a drink

WALTER MATTHAU
Walter Matthau reckons that he has lost over a million pounds gambling and once gambled a year's salary on the outcome of an exhibition baseball game. 'The worst moment I recall was back in 1958, when I was doing a television series. I bet $20,000 on the Yankees and they lost. I bet $80,000 on their second game and they lost one-nil. I went out and had a Scotch in Goldman's Bar across the street. Well, eighteen Scotches. I'd lost $100,000. I wasn't drunk, just petrified. I walked out into the sun feeling like a piece of cardboard.'

Ten stars who have been actively involved in politics

MELINA MERCOURI
Melina Mercouri was elected to the Greek Parliament as Member for the Piraeus in 1977. She later became Minister of Culture and Science.

PAUL NEWMAN
In 1968 Paul Newman campaigned full-time for US Presidential Candidate Eugene McCarthy. Ten years later he served as a delegate to the United Nations conference on disarmament.

GREGORY PECK
The Oscar-winning actor of *To Kill a Mockingbird* was put on a special danger list by the Nixon administration because of his radical liberal beliefs.

EDWARD ASNER
Television's 'Lou Grant' was elected President of the Screen Actors' Guild in 1981.

PEARL BAILEY
Black actress Pearl Bailey, best known for her performance in *Porgy and Bess*, was appointed Special Adviser to the United States Mission to the United Nations in 1975.

MARIE-FRANCE PISIER
This French actress, once labelled 'The thinking man's Bardot', campaigned for the Women's Liberation Movement and was actively involved in the 1968 student demonstrations in Paris.

PAUL ROBESON
The star of *Showboat* had his passport confiscated in 1950 because of his allegedly dangerous left-wing views, and not until 1958 could he collect the Stalin Peace Prize that he had been awarded six years earlier.

EDWARD G. ROBINSON
Edward G. Robinson's supposed Communist links led to his appearance before the House Un-American Activities Committee. Although he was cleared, his career suffered badly.

ROBERT RYAN
The star of *God's Little Acre* was a committed liberal who fought for the abolition of the House Un-American Activities Committee. He once said: 'I have been in films pretty well everything I am dedicated to fighting against.'

JANE FONDA
The daughter of Henry Fonda vehemently opposed the war in Vietnam and campaigned on behalf of underprivileged Indians.

Four stories in which Richard Burton plays a lead role

THE KNEE-SQUEEZE
When Richard Burton first arrived in Hollywood he went to a party at which Greta Garbo was also present. Burton sat down next to the 'Ice-Cool Goddess' and asked her: 'May I squeeze your knee?' but before the Swedish star could reply Burton had fulfilled his wish. He then smiled, bowed and left.

LONG WORDS
Elizabeth Taylor used to nag Richard Burton about his continual use of long words. At one London dinner party in consecutive sentences he came out with ramentaceous, spociferous and melonium. Then he said excrement. A fuming Elizabeth Taylor could stand no more and shouted in front of the other guests: 'Don't you think shit is a better word?'

DICK
Early in his career Burton was introduced at a party as 'Dick'. The Welshman recalled: 'I asked him if he would please call me Richard, Dick made me feel like a symbol of some kind.'

NOT JUST GOOD FRIENDS
Humphrey Bogart and Richard Burton once went up to a very respectable-looking lady at a Hollywood party and Bogart asked her: 'I've got to take a leak. Can you direct me to the men's room?' Burton winked and added: 'The real truth is that we are "that way" about each other and we need privacy.'

Eight stars who have served prison sentences

TOM NEAL
When Tom Neal's third wife was shot dead in 1965 the actor was convicted of manslaughter. He served a six-year prison sentence, dying just a few months after his release.

Sophia Loren

The Italian screen goddess spent a month in prison in 1982 for income tax irregularities.

Bobby Driscoll

Child star Bobby Driscoll was imprisoned in 1961 on a drugs charge. He later commented upon his tragic life: 'I was carried on a satin cushion and then dropped into a garbage car.' He died in 1968 at the age of thirty-two.

Walter Wanger

The producer of *Cleopatra* spent a period in prison in the early 1950s after shooting the agent of his wife, Joan Bennett, in a fit of jealousy.

Robert Mitchum

Robert Mitchum was jailed for two months for allegedly puffing on a joint of marijuana in 1948 at Laurel Canyon, USA.

Mae West

The most enduring sex-symbol the screen has ever known was briefly jailed in 1926 on account of her Broadway show *Sex*. The show that she wrote, produced and starred in was considered lewd.

Jane Russell

The star who once had the enviable billing 'Mean, Moody and Magnificent' was jailed on a drink driving charge in 1978 when she was fifty-seven.

Arletty

The French actress was arrested for collaboration with the Germans during the Second World War and was sentenced to two months in prison in 1945.

... And the Hollywood Ten

Alvah Bessie, Herbert Biberman, Lester Cole, Edward Dmytryk, Ring Lardner Junior, John Howard Lawson, Albert Maltz, Sam Ornitz, Adrian Scott and Dalton Trumbo were the famous band of writers, producers and directors who in 1947 refused to tell the Un-American Activities Committee whether or not they were Communists. They all served short prison sentences.

Four stars who have been successfully sued

DOUGLAS FAIRBANKS

In 1921 Douglas Fairbanks, in an effort to promote *Robin Hood*, posed on a New York rooftop with a bow and arrow. Unfortunately, the actor accidentally released the arrow and saw it fly across the street and lodge in a tailor's backside as he was sewing buttonholes. The man ran yelping into the street screaming about Red Indians. The incident cost Fairbanks $5,000 to settle out of court.

SONNY TUFTS

This American character actor was successfully sued by several showgirls who accused him of biting them in the thigh. The publicity didn't enhance his career and his name became a household joke.

LEE MARVIN

In 1979 Lee Marvin was sued by Michelle Triola Marvin, his lover for six years, for half his earnings during their time together, a sum which amounted to $1,800,000. The Judge awarded only $104,000.

MONTGOMERY CLIFT

Montgomery Clift sued Universal Studios for $200,000 over his fee for *Freud, the Secret Passion* (1963). In retaliation the studio counter-sued for nearly $700,000 because of Clift's heavy drinking. The matter was settled out of court.

Four people turned down for active service

RONALD REAGAN

Though Reagan entered the army in 1942 poor eyesight kept him out of action.

DONALD SINDEN

Donald Sinden was turned down for naval service in the Second World War because of his asthma.

MONTGOMERY CLIFT

Montgomery Clift was rejected by the army in the Second World War because he suffered from chronic diarrhoea.

NOEL COWARD

The archetypal Englishman was turned down by the army for the First World War because of a tubercular gland.

Four unfortunate faux pas

At a benefit for haemophilia Richard Burton told the audience that he had been a 'bleeder' all his life.

Peter O'Toole went to see Hollywood producer Sam Spiegel at the Connaught Hotel, London, to discuss the possibility of winning the title role in *Lawrence of Arabia*. On meeting Mr Spiegel, the Irish actor took off his coat and a bottle of whisky fell to the floor.

Comedian Bob Hope once joked on television: 'All schools in the Bronx will be closed tomorrow because it's Sal Mineo's birthday.' The next day nobody went to school in the Bronx.

Joe Grossman, studio manager of the Elstree Studios in the 1930s, was giving the King of Greece a conducted tour. 'In this film, your Majesty, we are using the 'abitats of a café – the camera is put inside the box cos we don't want to 'ear anything, and the thing up there on a pole is a boom and the sound goes through the air . . . but I expect this is all Greek to you . . .'

Thirty dates to remember

1932   Corinne Griffith retires to devote herself to 'real estate, Christian Science and the abolition of income tax'.

1933   Fred Astaire dances on film for the first time in *Flying Down to Rio*.

1934   A department of amusement is added to the US President's cabinet.

1935   Issur Danielovich Demsky, later known as Kirk Douglas, wins Inter-Collegiate Wrestling Championship.

1936   Elizabeth Taylor goes to kindergarten for the first time.

1937   Kirk Douglas, Peter Finch, Anthony Quinn and Victor Mature celebrate their twenty-first birthdays.

1938   Bob Hope makes his film début in *The Big Broadcast*.

1941   *Fortune* magazine discovers that 79 per cent of the US population prefers listening to the radio to going to the cinema.

1942   Errol Flynn arrested and subsequently acquitted on four charges of statutory rape.

1945   Steve McQueen becomes a merchant seaman.

1948   James Dean wins Indiana State dramatic contest doing a monologue.

1951   Betty Grable is the number one female box office attraction in the United States with Doris Day a close second.

1952   Stewart Granger is named in a poll as the most unpopular Englishman in Hollywood.

1953   Shirley Maclaine, Alan Bates and Brigitte Bardot celebrate their eighteenth birthdays.

1956   Marilyn Monroe marries dramatist Arthur Miller.

1959   David Niven, at last, wins Best Actor Oscar for *Separate Tables*.

1961   Bobby Darin buys a car worth $150,000. It is partly painted with crushed diamond dust.

1962   Jane Fonda is made Miss Army Recruitment.

1963   Sean Connery receives $15,000 for his first Bond movie, *Dr No*.

1964   Omar Sharif represents Egypt in the 1964 Olympic Bridge Tournament.

1966   Cary Grant becomes a father for the first time at the age of sixty-two.

1968   Warren Beatty is a member of John Glenn's Emergency Gun Controls Committee.

1972   Frankie Howerd gets stuck in a lift with Raquel Welch at a hotel in Budapest.

1974   Steve McQueen is made an Honorary Los Angeles Fire Fighter.

1975   Elizabeth Taylor wins and Richard Burton is runner-up in The *Observer* Readers' list of bores.

1977   Charlton Heston is awarded the Jean Hershott Humanitarian Award.

1979   The last of the Marx Brothers, Zeppo, dies.

1981   Tatum O'Neal celebrates her eighteenth birthday.

1984   Richard Burton dies soon after completing Orwell's *1984*.

1985   Lee Remick, Woody Allen and Burt Reynolds celebrate their fiftieth birthdays.

Five origins of names and catchphrases

BRONSON
Charles Buchinski was driving down Hollywood Boulevard when he came to a red light, stopped, looked to his right and saw that the name of the street was Bronson. Impressed, he promptly changed his name.

'OSCAR'
'The Oscar' is so named, reputedly, because when the figure was made in 1927 a secretary said: 'It reminds me of my Uncle Oscar.'

WHAT'S NEW PUSSYCAT?
Producer Charles Feldman chose the film title *What's New Pussycat?* after he'd had Warren Beatty staying with him in Manhattan. Beatty would ring his numerous girlfriends always opening with the line 'What's new Pussycat?'

ANYONE FOR TENNIS?

Surprisingly, Humphrey Bogart is generally believed to be partly responsible for this phrase. In the early days of his career he uttered the line 'Tennis anyone?' in a little-known play off Broadway.

ANNIE HALL

Actress Diane Keaton's real name is Diane Hall. Hence her Oscar-winning role in Woody Allen's *Annie Hall*.

... And three people particular about their own names

Peter Finch insisted that his name should be pronounced 'Fink'.

Warren Beatty is convinced that the correct pronunciation of his name is 'Badey'.

Lauren Bacall prefers to be addressed by her real name, 'Betty Pepske'.

Four stars who have suffered embarrassing experiences

SIR JOHN GIELGUD

When Clement Attlee was Prime Minister, Sir John Gielgud was asked to dine with him at a hotel in Stratford upon Avon, Warwickshire. Sir John sat next to Mr Attlee's daughter. They were discussing where they lived. 'I have a very convenient home in Westminster,' Sir John remarked, 'and where do you live?' A startled Miss Attlee replied: 'Number Ten Downing Street.'

ERROL FLYNN

On the day or morning of his wedding in Nice, France, to Patrice Wymore, Errol Flynn was handed a document accusing him of the rape of a French girl named Denise Duvivier.

VINCENT PRICE

Vincent Price once did a US television series on cooking. It has the reputation of being the most embarrassing series in the history of the small screen.

WALTER MATTHAU

Walter Matthau was walking down a street in New York when he was approached by a woman. 'You are Walter Matthau, aren't you?' she asked. Matthau nodded in agreement. 'They make you look much younger in the movies,' she told him.

Ten stars born in London

Dirk Bogarde
Michael Caine
Peter Finch
Stewart Granger
Sir Alec Guinness
Oliver Reed
Vanessa Redgrave
Jean Simmons
Elizabeth Taylor
Susannah York

Five first meetings

ROMAIN GARY AND CLINT EASTWOOD

Romain Gary, novelist husband of actress Jean Seberg, was so enraged by reports of an affair between his wife and Clint Eastwood on the set of *Paint Your Wagon* that he flew to the States from his home in France. He confronted the actor at five in the morning in the kitchen of Alan Jay Lerner's cabin and threatened to murder the star unless he left his wife alone. Mr Eastwood's reaction is not recorded.

FRANKIE HOWERD AND MICHAEL WINNER

In 1962 Frankie Howerd was making *The Cool Mikado* under the direction of the extrovert British director, Michael Winner. The comedian recalls that when they were first introduced the self-effacing Mr Winner told him: 'You must understand that I'm a genius.'

RAY MILLAND AND CLARA BOW

In the early days of his Hollywood career Welshman Ray Milland was slightly taken aback when at a smart party he was approached by the vivacious Clara Bow who said: 'Hi, don't drink the Scotch, it will kill you. Take the gin, it might not.'

IAN FLEMING AND SEAN CONNERY

When Ian Fleming, writer of the Bond books, first met Sean Connery, he was unimpressed and said: 'I'm looking for Commander James Bond, not an overgrown stunt man.'

DOROTHY SPENCE ON HUSBAND ROBERT MITCHUM

Dorothy Spence was not terribly taken by the man she was later to marry, Robert Mitchum, when they first met. 'To be perfectly honest, I didn't like him. He was a wise guy. He never thought of paying a compliment like other boys, preferring to tease.'

Ten public schoolboys

Stewart Granger	*Epsom College*
Charles Laughton	*Stonyhurst College*
James Mason	*Marlborough*

Daniel Massey	*Eton College*
Robert Morley	*Wellington College*
David Niven	*Stowe*
Sir Anthony Quayle	*Rugby*
Basil Rathbone	*Repton*
Peter Ustinov	*Westminster*
Simon Ward	*Alleyn's School*

Five things you perhaps didn't know about Gone With the Wind

1 It took three years to make.
2 Thirteen screen writers and three directors were employed at some stage on the making of the film.
3 It cost four million dollars to make.
4 475,000 feet of film were shot.
5 On the day of the première in Atlanta, Georgia, the streets were lined for seven miles with people wanting to pay homage to Clark Gable and Vivien Leigh.

Five stars who met a strange end

WILLIAM HOLDEN
In November 1981 William Holden was discovered lying in a pool of blood beside his bed. He had been dead for several days. The Coroner's report stated that he had fallen, struck his head on the bedside table and bled to death – too drunk to call for help.

JAMES WHALE
The English director responsible for *Frankenstein* (1931) and

Showboat was found drowned in his own swimming pool in 1957.

FRANK SILVERA
The actor best known for his TV performance in *The High Chaparral*, who later became professor of drama at California State University, met his end when he accidentally electrocuted himself at his home in 1970.

JACK CASSIDY
The father of the singer David Cassidy was killed in a fire in 1976, probably started by a cigarette. It took five fire departments to put out the blaze. His body was identified by medical records.

A.J. BAKANAS
When the famous stunt man was filming *Steel* in 1979 he jumped off a building over three hundred feet high. Though he landed on a crash pad he broke the top seam and went through the top of the bag, and the second layer alone wasn't enough to save him.

Ten unusual facts

1 The combined cost of the highly successful *Airplane* and *Friday the Thirteenth* was less than the cost of the closing credit titles of the *Star Trek* movie in 1979.

2 In the silent movie days the average professional stuntman's life was about five years.

3 Cary Grant married Barbara Harris in Frank Sinatra's Palm Springs home in 1981.

4   Using the United States government's cost of living index, if you were going to film *Cleopatra* in 1985 it would cost well over $110 million. It cost $44 million in 1962.

5   Three times more film stars die violent deaths than sports stars. Ten per cent of the top movie stars die tragically.

6   The word 'Paris' appears in more film titles than any other word except 'love'.

7   With the exception of *Rebecca* it was not until the 1960s that a thriller won the Best Picture Oscar.

8   Howard Hughes hired Oscar Milland to write the screenplay for *The Conqueror* even though Milland admitted that he couldn't even spell Genghis Khan.

9   Squeaky-voiced Madeline Kahn (*What's Up Doc?*, *Young Frankenstein*) has a degree in speech therapy.

10 There were two life stories of Oscar Wilde in 1960, two life stories of Jean Harlow in 1965 and three 1976 accounts of the Israeli raid on Entebbe Airport.

Five stars who died from drugs

Nigel Green
The British character actor who gave notable performances in *The Ipcress File* and *Tobruk* died of an accidental overdose of sleeping pills at the age of forty-eight.

Margaret Sullivan
The first wife of Henry Fonda took an overdose of barbiturates when she was forty-nine because she believed she was going deaf.

JOHN BELUSHI
The plump star of *National Lampoon's Animal House* and *The Blues Brothers* died from a drugs overdose at the age of thirty-three.

PIER ANGELI
The Sardinian-born actress, once romantically linked with James Dean, died from an overdose of barbiturates whilst making a Hollywood comeback in *Octamon*, aged thirty-nine.

JEAN SEBERG
The American leading lady of *Saint Joan* was found dead, in her car, from an overdose of barbiturates. She had been there a week and nobody had reported her missing.

Four leading ladies who were not above delivering a bitchy remark

ELIZABETH TAYLOR
Debbie Reynolds had married Eddie Fisher in 1955. By 1959 Elizabeth Taylor had become a major part of Mr Fisher's life, and in that year he left Debbie Reynolds for the twenty-seven-year-old English star. Elizabeth Taylor remarked about the triangle: 'I'm not taking anything away from Debbie Reynolds because she never really had it.'

GREER GARSON
As Joan Crawford stood appreciating the applause after the première of *Mildred Pierce* in 1945, Greer Garson turned to her and said: 'Well, none of us should be surprised. After all, my dear, you are a tradition.'

JULIE ANDREWS
When Julie Andrews starred with Rock Hudson in *Darling Lili* in 1970, gossip columnist Joyce Haber reported that Miss

Andrews repeatedly reminded her co-star: 'Remember, I'm the leading lady.'

KATHARINE HEPBURN

After working with Robert Mitchum in 1946 on *Undercurrent* Katharine Hepburn told Mitchum: 'You know you can't act, and if you hadn't been good-looking you would never have got a picture. I'm tired of playing with people who have nothing to offer.'

... And one actress who had an unusual gift delivered

On gossip columnist Hedda Hopper's birthday Joan Bennett bought a skunk that had been dead for a week, put it into a shoebox, wrapped it up and had it delivered to Miss Hopper with the message 'Happy Birthday, dear, Joan.'

Ten successful films that were made into TV series

Casablanca
Batman
Mash
The Asphalt Jungle
The Saint
Dr Kildare
Shaft
National Velvet
The Planet of the Apes
The Odd Couple

Thirteen stars discuss themselves

JOAN COLLINS

'I'm a very shy woman, very sensitive, very emotional, very volatile, with quite a sense of humour. I care deeply about my friends, but because of my vulnerable streak I compensate by seeming much tougher.'

JIMMY STEWART

'When they get round to writing my epitaph I'll settle for, I'll be happy with: "He sure gave us a lot of pleasure over the years."'

FRANKIE HOWERD

'I suppose that the best that could be said of me is that he means well.'

BURT LANCASTER

'Deep down I'm a frustrated opera singer.

'Most people seem to think I'm the kind of guy who shaves with a blow-torch. Actually I'm inclined to be bookish and worrisome.'

BOB HOPE

'I'm such a ham. Somebody said that if I were in a blizzard and two Eskimo dogs walked by, I'd do ten minutes for them. But I'm not the kind of guy who's on all the time either. I don't want to be on all the time.'

MICHAEL WILDING

'I was the worst actor I ever came across.'

KATHARINE HEPBURN

'When I started out I didn't have any desire to be an actress or to learn how to act. I just wanted to be a star.'

CHARLES BRONSON
'I hardly every see my own films. I don't like the look of myself or the way I speak. I'm surprised the public likes me.
  'I have lots of friends and yet I don't have any.'

BRIGITTE BARDOT
'On the outside one is a star. But in reality, one is completely alone, doubting everything. To experience this loneliness of soul is the hardest thing in the world.'

BILL HOLDEN
'I'm a whore, all actors are whores. We sell our bodies to the highest bidder. I had practice being a whore when I was a young actor starting out in Hollywood. I used to service actresses who were older than me.'

RITA HAYWORTH
'I haven't had everything from life. I've had too much.'

PETER O'TOOLE
'I can't stand light. I hate weather. My idea of heaven is moving from one smoke-filled room to another. I never go out in the fresh air at home.'

JAMES DEAN
'I'm terribly gauche and so tense I don't see how people stay in the same room with me. I know I wouldn't tolerate myself.'

Their first screen kiss

Elizabeth Taylor	by James Lydon in *Cynthia*.
Deborah Kerr	by Clifford Evans in *Love on the Dole*.
Bonita Granville	by William Holden in *Those Were the Days*.
Mary Pickford (aged thirty-four)	by Budge Rogers in *My Best Girl*.

Deanna Durbin	by Robert Stack in *Three Smart Girls Grow Up*.
Clint Eastwood	by Carol Channing in *The First Travelling Saleslady*.

Nicknames

Florence Lawrence	*'Biograph Girl'*.
Clara Bow	*'The It Girl'*.
Betty Grable	*'The Pin-up Girl'*.
Anne Sheridan	*'The Oomph Girl'*.
Lana Turner	*'The Sweater Girl'*.
Florence Turner	*'The Vitagraph Girl'*.
Jean Harlow	*'The Platinum Blonde'*.
Lon Chaney	*'The Man of a Thousand Faces'*.
Jeanne Eagels	*'Gin Eagels'*.

And when Marilyn Monroe and Sir Laurence Olivier co-starred in *The Prince and the Showgirl* one critic nicknamed them 'The Knight and the Garter'.

Three stars who have lost their temper

STEWART GRANGER
When gossip columnist Hedda Hopper accused Michael Wilding, husband of Elizabeth Taylor, of being a homosexual, Stewart Granger rang her up and said:

'I just called up to say that I think you're a monumental bitch. How bloody dare you call a friend of mine a queer, you raddled up, dried up, frustrated old cunt.'

PETER O'TOOLE

After co-starring with Peter O'Toole in *Man of La Mancha*, Sophia Loren's next film was *The Journey* with Richard Burton. O'Toole wrote to her from London: 'The news is all over Ireland that I am spitting blood at the moon, aghast because you have abandoned me for a bandy-legged pock-marked little Welshman.'

CARY GRANT

Dyan Cannon tells the story that when she was married to Cary Grant they were watching the Academy Awards one year in their bedroom with a few friends and: 'He became violent and out of control. He jumped up and down on the bed. This lasted for a couple of hours – as long as the awards were on.'

Fifteen real names of the stars

Mary Astor	*Lucille Langhanke.*
Charles Bronson	*Charles Buchinsky.*
Joan Crawford	*Lucille de Sueur.*
Bob Hope	*Leslie Townes Hope.*
Rock Hudson	*Roy Scherer.*
Hedy Lamarr	*Hedwig Kiesler.*
Walter Matthau	*Walter Matuschanskayasky.*
Ray Milland	*Reginald Alfred John Truscott-Jones.*
Mary Pickford	*Gladys Smith.*
Stephanie Powers	*Stefania Zofja Federkievicz.*
Martin Sheen	*Ramon Estevez.*
Robert Taylor	*Spangler Arlington Brough.*
Twiggy	*Lesley Hornsby.*
Rudolph Valentino	*Rodolpho Alfonso Rafaelo Filibert Guglielmi di Valentina.*
John Wayne	*Marion Robert Morrison.*

Ten unlikely priests

Richard Burton	*Becket.*
Montgomery Clift	*I Confess.*
William Holden	*Satan Never Sleeps.*
Trevor Howard	*Ryan's Daughter.*
Karl Malden	*On the Waterfront.*
Oliver Reed	*The Devils.*
Mickey Rooney	*The Twinkle in God's Eye.*
Patrick Troughton	*The Omen.*
Frank Sinatra	*The Miracle of the Bells.*
David Warner	*The Ballad of Cable Hogue.*

One who went all the way to Pope

Anthony Quinn	*The Shoes of the Fisherman.*

... And one who went right to the top

George Burns	*Oh God.*

Five stars who weren't terribly well bred

Greta Garbo	Father was a Stockholm labourer.
Clint Eastwood	Father was a gas-station attendant.
Anthony Quinn	Father was an Irish fruit picker.
Charlie Chaplin	Father was an alcoholic. His mother suffered from mental illness.
Michael Caine	Father was a fishmarket porter. His mother was a charlady.

Three reasons why Tony Curtis and Jack Lemmon didn't get on with Marilyn Monroe on the set of *Some Like it Hot*

Marilyn took forty takes to utter the words: 'Where is that Bourbon?'

Tony Curtis and Jack Lemmon, dressed as women, are in the bedroom. There is a knock on the door. One of them says 'Yes', to which Marilyn replies: 'It's me, Sugar.'

There were forty-seven takes. After thirty takes, Marilyn's line was put on a blackboard for her to read.

During one scene, Tony Curtis had to chew a chicken bone for forty-two takes because Marilyn couldn't remember her lines. Curtis lost his appetite for chicken for months afterwards.

Ten crucial pieces of advice from the stars

CLARK GABLE
'Stick to the Scotch if you want to be brave. Gin only makes you piss.'

BILL HOLDEN (TO PETER FINCH)
'Take any picture you can. One out of five will be good, one out of ten will be very good, and one out of fifteen will get you an Academy Award.'

CARY GRANT
'Never have any doubts. Always believe whatever you want will be there.'

CHARLIE CHAPLIN (TO DAVID NIVEN)
'Don't be like the great majority of actors ... Don't just stand around waiting your turn to speak – learn to listen.'

BOB HOPE
'Timing is the essence of life and definitely comedy.'

FRANKIE HOWERD
'Take one's work seriously, but not oneself.'

ERROL FLYNN (TO PETER FINCH)
'You're acting! Don't act! I don't act, that's why I'm a star.'

JOHN WAYNE
'When you are with small people, sit down quietly so they can tower over you. It makes them feel good.'

BURT LANCASTER
'Life is to be lived within the limits of your knowledge and within the concept of what you would like to see yourself to be.'

ALFRED HITCHCOCK
'I deny I ever said that actors are cattle. What I said was that actors should be treated like cattle.'